BUILDING A FOLDING
Model Railway Layout
A COMPREHENSIVE GUIDE

To complement this night scene, the First Great Western DMU model, retailed by Dapol, is fitted with an optional carriage lighting kit.

BUILDING A FOLDING
Model Railway Layout

A COMPREHENSIVE GUIDE

GRAHAM GOODCHILD

THE CROWOOD PRESS

First published in 2016 by
The Crowood Press Ltd
Ramsbury, Marlborough
Wiltshire SN8 2HR

www.crowood.com

British Library Cataloguing-in-Publication Data
A catalogue record for this book is available from the British Library.

ISBN 978 1 78500 199 4

Dedication
For Lily and Eleanor

Acknowledgements
My thanks go to the Technical Advice Bureau at Peco for their help in providing information
on track wiring for the layout featured in this book. Also, thank you to Expressway Models,
South Devon Railway for allowing me to photograph their model railway items. I am also
indebted to the many feature writers, editors and contributors of various model railway
magazines who have given me inspiration to build my own layout. Last, but certainly not
least, a big thank you to my family and friends for their interest and support throughout the
construction of the featured layout and during the writing of this book.

Disclaimer
The author and the publisher do not accept any responsibility in any manner whatsoever for
any error or omission, or any loss, damage, injury, adverse outcome, or liability of any kind
incurred as a result of the use of any of the information contained in this book, or reliance
upon it. If in doubt about any aspect of railway modelling readers are advised to seek
professional advice.

Typeset by Jean Cussons Typesetting, Diss, Norfolk
Printed and bound in Malaysia by Times Offset (M) Sdn Bhd

CONTENTS

INTRODUCTION

My interest in designing and constructing working models, including radio-controlled models, spans more than sixty years and started at a tender age with the gift of a penknife. Many a happy hour was spent whittling away at any old piece of scrap wood I could find, usually resulting in some sort of model boat of dubious description.

For one reason or another, model trains have not been one of my modelling priorities. Indeed, up to recently, my only experience of model trains had been a Triang train set received as a boy one Christmas. I remember that I would delight in seeing how fast I could make the train take a curve before it parted company with the track and the locomotive, predictably, coming to grief against a chair leg or some other item of household furniture. I now look back in horror at my disrespectful treatment of this once pristine model railway.

Now living near a main-line railway, I would sometimes stop on my way into town and watch the trains go by. The sight and sound of the Intercity diesels thundering past inspired me to build myself a proper model railway that would enable me to sit back and watch the trains go by and perhaps be entertained by incorporating some additional working features within the layout.

I think one of the reasons why I didn't venture into model railways until recently was space, or rather the lack of it. Modern houses are not always over-generous in size and so a train layout sometimes cannot be out on permanent display. Also, the layout had to be large enough to accommodate one or more oval tracks for the continuous running of trains. It was this that led me to believe that what I required was a layout that could be folded and stored away when not in use. Traditionally a type of fibreboard is used for the base of layouts. However, as the folding layout needed to be portable, and in order to reduce weight, I decided that

Fig. I   The folding layout – Teignside Quay.

lightweight foam should be used for the base and the landscaping.

This comprehensive guide shows, with instructions, photographs and diagrams, how to construct a complete portable tabletop or stand-alone folding layout from timber and lightweight materials, such as foam. It also describes the techniques used in its construction. Most of the techniques considered in this book can equally be applied to other model railway layouts and scales. The base of the featured layout has sides and folds in half in a similar way to a large suitcase, thus keeping dirt and dust out (which can be a real nuisance with small-scale models) and, importantly, protecting the layout when stored away.

The featured layout is constructed to N-gauge scale and can accommodate up to three trains running simultaneously on tracks that run under and over hills surrounding a central water feature with boats moored to the quayside and paddle-boarders in action. Working features include a cable car and rolling road, together with a children's roundabout and a helicopter with rotating blades. Construction details are described for these, including making street lighting, lighting for buildings and vehicles using LEDs and fibre optics for special effects. This book also describes what tools and adhesives are required, materials and their use, how to lay the track, wiring and landscaping.

It is intended that this book will appeal not only to modellers who wish to build the featured layout, but also will provide ideas for designing and building your own layout.

CHAPTER ONE

FIRST THOUGHTS

RESEARCH

Not having built what I would call a 'proper' model railway before, I was unsure where I should start. In hindsight it would have been advantageous if I had joined my local model railway club, where no doubt I would have been put on the right track and also would have gained some valuable experience.

It was only by chance upon visiting a heritage railway, in the model shop located within the train station, that I came across some small model locomotives and carriages. These locomotives were half the size of the OO-scale trains that I had been previously accustomed to as a youngster. I learned that these small locomotives were in fact N-gauge scale; apparently N-gauge model railways have been

around for more than forty years. I certainly had a lot of catching up to do regarding the availability of products and it was also going to be a steep learning curve in the construction of a model railway layout.

My local newsagent was my first port of call in my quest for what magazines had to offer on model railways, and certainly seeing the number of different titles seemed to testify to the popularity of the subject. I came away with a handful of magazines to take home and study, the majority of which helpfully show how to make various layout features. Also, the advertisements in the magazines are a helpful source of products that are available to the railway modeller. Going online and trawling through the seemingly endless websites is also a great source of information for everything on the subject; this

Fig. 2 Online research and gleaning information from magazines on the world of model railways is a good place to start when deciding on the type of layout to build.

Fig. 3   The gauge scales diagram shows the different sizes of the four main scales.

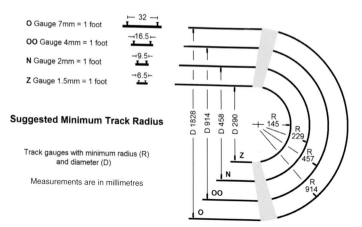

O Gauge 7mm = 1 foot

OO Gauge 4mm = 1 foot

N Gauge 2mm = 1 foot

Z Gauge 1.5mm = 1 foot

Suggested Minimum Track Radius

Track gauges with minimum radius (R) and diameter (D)

Measurements are in millimetres

eventually pointed me in the right direction on the kind of layout that I wanted to build.

SIZE MATTERS

The four main sizes, or gauges to be precise, in model railways range from O gauge down to the smallest at Z gauge. Of the four main sizes, OO gauge is the most popular, closely followed by N gauge.

O GAUGE

This gauge represents a scale of 7mm to 1ft and a track gauge of 32mm measured across the rails. Due to its size, this gauge requires plenty of space, especially if a circular or an oval layout is contemplated. The minimum recommended radius for O gauge is approximately 914mm (36in). Therefore, a circular layout would occupy a space of at least 2m (7ft) square. A folding layout of this size and weight may be impractical, even for the most muscle-bound amongst us. However, a single-track siding of about 2m in length, depicting a scale dock or factory scene, for example, would be feasible as this could be constructed in two sections, making a manageable package for transportation and storage.

OO GAUGE

This gauge represents a scale of 4mm to 1ft and a track gauge of 16.5mm. As an aside, HO gauge is the US and Continental equivalent of OO gauge; although slightly smaller than OO gauge, both these gauges share the same track gauge of 16.5mm.

N GAUGE

N gauge represents a scale of 2mm to 1ft and a track gauge of 9.5mm, and has the advantage that up to four times the amount of track and scenery can be built in the same space that an OO-gauge layout would occupy. From a modelling point of view, N gauge is probably the smallest gauge to which lineside and other small items, such as working street lighting, can still be fairly easily made and is the choice of gauge for Teignside Quay, the layout featured in this book.

Z GAUGE

Z gauge represents a scale of 1.5mm to 1ft and a track gauge of 6.5mm. The possibilities are almost endless with this gauge, from a simple rigid layout housed in a desk drawer to a multi-track setting running through vistas of rolling hills and mountain scenery. However, making working features and the electrical connections between numerous track circuits at this small scale would be challenging, though not impossible.

The OO, N and Z gauges are certainly suitable for circular or oval-type folding layouts. An OO-gauge, single-track circular layout incorporating a small siding, for example, could quite easily be

Fig. 4   Not much larger than a ballpoint pen, the N-gauge Class A1 Tornado is flanked at the top by an OO-gauge Royal Scot and at the bottom by the diminutive Z-gauge Flying Scotsman.

accommodated within the size of the folding base-board described in this book.

All the above gauges are well catered for with products manufactured by various companies, including track, locomotives and rolling stock, together with landscaping materials, lineside items, buildings, vehicles and figures. When building a folding layout, consideration has to be given in the design to the height of any elevated sections of track, which includes hills, buildings and trees, if the layout is to close shut without damaging the contents.

DESIGN CONSIDERATIONS

This section considers the approach used in designing my own folding N-gauge layout and describes the drawing aides required, which may be of interest if you wish to have a go at designing your own layout.

Also described are suggested drawing scales, choice of track, controllers and design of the folding box.

DRAWING AIDS

Making rough preliminary sketches of your ideas on track layout, scenery and positions of working features will be of help on your final plan, for which you will require a sheet of preferably A3-size graph paper marked in 1cm or 1in squares. This will help you to draw straight lines and will assist in measuring. Other items required are a pencil, eraser, metric- or imperial-scale ruler and a pair of compasses and dividers.

SCALE OF DRAWINGS

The maximum size scale of drawing for small to medium-size layouts that will fit within A3-size paper is 1:5 metric scale. In other words, twenty 1cm squares on the paper represent 1m full size.

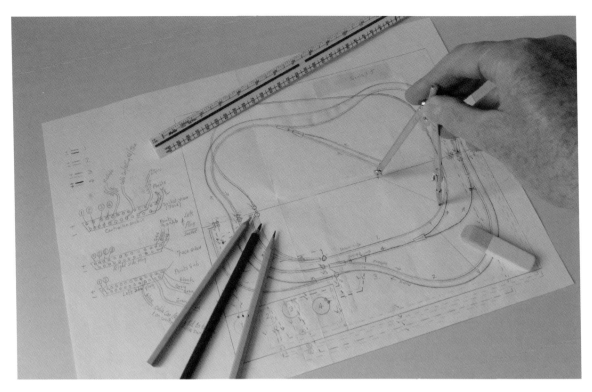

Fig. 5   Basic drawing instruments are all that is required for putting your ideas onto paper. Coloured pencils are also useful to determine where track wiring should be located.

Therefore, for example, a layout size measuring up to 1.8 × 1.4m will fit on the A3 paper.

For working in imperial measurements, a scale of 2in to 1ft would be suitable; for example, a layout size measuring up to 7 × 5ft could also be accommodated on A3-size paper.

ON TRACK

The next things to consider are choice of track gauge and type of track to be used, together with the number of continuous circuits, sidings and passing loops, and so on. For Teignside Quay, the folding layout featured in this book, I used flexi-track manufactured by Peco. Flexi-track is available in 1m (3ft) lengths and, as the name suggests, it can be bent by hand to form whatever radius is required. It is particularly useful where realistic, gentle, transitional curves are required. Flexi-track usually has to be permanently fixed to the baseboard.

Set-track, on the other hand, consists of short lengths of straight and curved sections of track of various radii that clip together. This type of track is useful for temporary layouts and can easily be extended by adding more sections of track. This track can also be permanently fixed in place, if required.

POINTS

Also sometimes referred to as 'turnouts', points are available in two types: insulfrog or electrofrog. The first type refers to the short, plastic, insulated nose section where the rails form a point and are normally used with set-track. With electrofrog points the pointed nose section is not insulated and its advantage is that it helps to prevent short-wheelbase locomotives from stalling on the points. However, both the insulfrog and electrofrog points have different electrical characteristics on the remaining

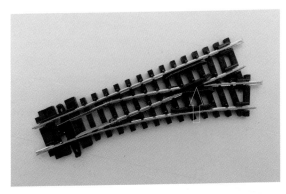

Fig. 6   A typical insulfrog turnout produced by Peco used mainly with set-track. Here the pointed nose section is made from black insulated plastic, unlike electrofrog turnouts where the pointed nose section is metal and is not insulated.

track. Detailed explanations on this are provided in other publications, which are listed in Appendix I at the end of this book.

The purpose of a folding layout, of course, is that it should be manageable and reasonably compact when folded. For multi-track circular or oval-type layouts, compactness may come at the expense of not being able to have long, sweeping curves and, therefore, minimum radius curves are required. This is not a problem with most locomotives and rolling stock, although perhaps an A1 class 'Tornado' steam locomotive pulling a rake of seven carriages in OO or N gauge, for example, may not look right on such tight curves and could be chasing its tail on smaller layouts. However, this should not be a problem with Z gauge, where more space can be made available.

Where flexi-track or set-track is to cross the baseboard joint on a folding layout, draw the outline of the track on your design plan straight and at right angles (90 degrees) to the baseboard joint. This will make it easier to align and fasten the track at the track-laying stage and facilitate the ends of the track joining together correctly when the layout is unfolded and fastened.

IN CONTROL

There are two systems for controlling locomotives on the track: analogue and digital command control (DCC). Both these systems provide electrical power to the track.

Digital Command Control (DCC)

This system is a fairly recent innovation and enables diesel or steam sounds, together with lighting, to be regulated on locomotives by a DCC controller. Moreover, the modeller also has the ability to use the DCC to control independently more than one locomotive on the same section of track. Locomotives can come already fitted with micro-decoder modules for operating the lighting and sound features, although decoder modules are also available separately for converting suitable analogue locomotives to DCC. It is possible to control DCC locomotives on analogue layouts but the lighting and sound features cannot be controlled by an analogue controller.

Analogue Control

This is probably the most recognizable method of controlling a model railway from past years. I remember my first layout came with a 12V mains transformer, the size and weight of a house brick, with a somewhat crude, separate, scratchily working controller; although I did enjoy hitting the red emergency stop button for those wheel-locking, skidding brake stops.

Nowadays analogue controllers are much more refined with excellent, slow-running capabilities, and are available for single-track and up to a four-track locomotive control. For the Teignside Quay layout I chose a four-track Gaugemaster analogue controller fitted with four independent speed controllers with reversing switches.

The fourth speed controller on the unit is used for controlling the working features on the layout. The 240V mains transformer is housed within the case of the controller together with a screw-type connection terminal block located on the back of the unit for attaching the wiring to the track, and comprises of 4 × 12V DC for the tracks, 2 × 12V DC and 2 × 16V AC for accessories, which are used for powering the lighting and working features on the layout.

Fig. 7   This analogue controller, manufactured by Gaugemaster, will control up to four locomotives on different tracks.

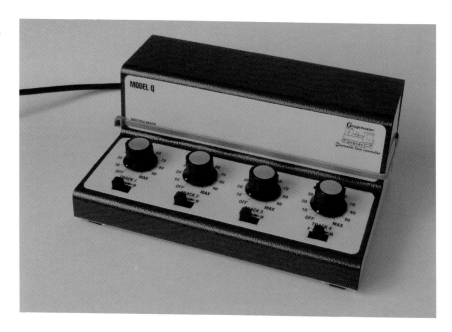

THE FOLDING BOX

My first thoughts on the folding-box concept had been triggered by my distant memory of seeing a very small-scale model railway layout housed in a suitcase. I thought at the time that this was a really neat idea and promised myself that one day I would have a go at building something similar. Fast forward to the present and, having decided to build an N-gauge layout with three-track circuits, I would require a very large suitcase indeed in which to accommodate the layout. The suitcase would need to have large holes cut out in the sides for access to the track under the hill structures, or the layout designed to be lifted out from the suitcase, which would require strengthening to carry the weight of a large layout. After much thought I decided to construct a tailor-made folding box.

The next consideration was the size of the layout within the folding box and the choice of materials to be used in its construction. Size also equates to the weight of the completed layout, which needs to be portable and also of a suitable size for storage. Model railway layouts are usually constructed on a composite fibre-board base, such as Sundeala, which is glued and screwed to a rigid timber frame. However, in order to keep weight to a minimum, I chose Styrofoam for the baseboard and the raised landscaping. Styrofoam is an extremely lightweight, rigid foam that is easy to cut and shape, although it was necessary to devise a method of fastening turnout motors and other lineside items directly to the foam base. After some experimentation, I came up with a workable method that is explained in Chapter 3.

The part of the layout known as the folding box or carcass is constructed from plywood with a conventional timber frame for supporting the foam base. The sides of the folding box slope down from the back towards the front. This allows adequate depth at the back for the viaduct and elevated section of track and ease of access to the front of the layout and train controller unit.

Legless or Standing

I wanted the layout to be versatile so that it could either be freestanding on its own, bolted on legs, or these could be removed for placing the layout on a tabletop. Additionally, I wanted the option of positioning the train controller unit on a foldable shelf arrangement underneath the layout to allow more space for track and additional features, if required.

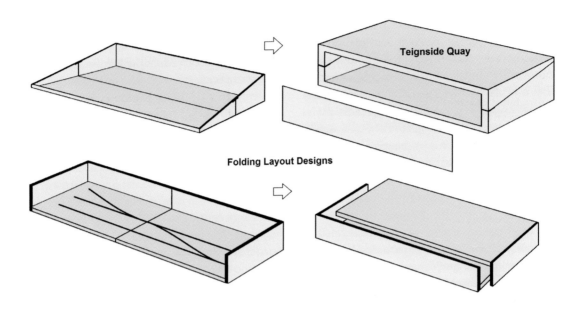

Teignside Quay

Folding Layout Designs

ABOVE: **Fig. 8** **Two examples of folding layouts. The top layout is the basic design for Teignside Quay, while the bottom design is suggested for a siding- or terminus-type layout.**

BELOW: **Fig. 9** **Buckfastleigh Station on the South Devon Railway. This station would make a suitable subject for a folding terminus layout.**

WORKING FEATURES

My first thoughts about the working features on the layout were somewhat over-ambitious to say the least. On my original wish-list I wanted a working cable car, rolling road, narrow-gauge railway and a water feature with actual water, using a pump from a goldfish aquarium. In reality a water droplet would be the size of a person's head in an N-gauge figure, and thus not at all realistic. Also, water and electricity is a dangerous mix, even though the layout voltage is only 12V. A far safer alternative is to make a water feature from a clear, hard-setting resin.

Using street lighting and lighting in buildings would add another dimension by giving a night-time atmosphere to the layout. Road vehicles could be modified to accept thin fibre-optic cables for working headlights and for special effects.

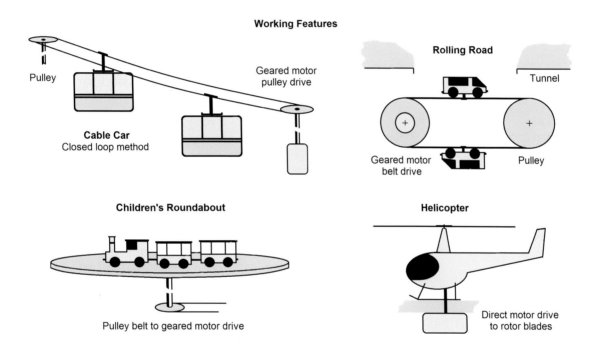

Working Features

Pulley

Geared motor pulley drive

Cable Car
Closed loop method

Rolling Road

Tunnel

Geared motor belt drive

Pulley

Children's Roundabout

Pulley belt to geared motor drive

Helicopter

Direct motor drive to rotor blades

Fig. 10   Ideas for working features, although the rolling road was rejected for a simpler arrangement.

CHAPTER TWO

TOOLS AND ADHESIVES

TOOLS

Tools can be divided into two categories: tools for constructing the folding layout, including the base and the folding-box arrangement, and modelling tools for track-laying, landscaping, lineside items, static and working features. You may be fortunate in already having a comprehensive selection of tools, in which case you are welcome to skip this section.

However, it has given me an excuse to clean up or replace some of my well-worn tools, which I list and illustrate here in case you may appreciate guidance on what tools are required.

TOOLS FOR MAKING THE FOLDING-BOX ARRANGEMENT

The tools required for marking out and cutting the lengths of timber for the base framework, together

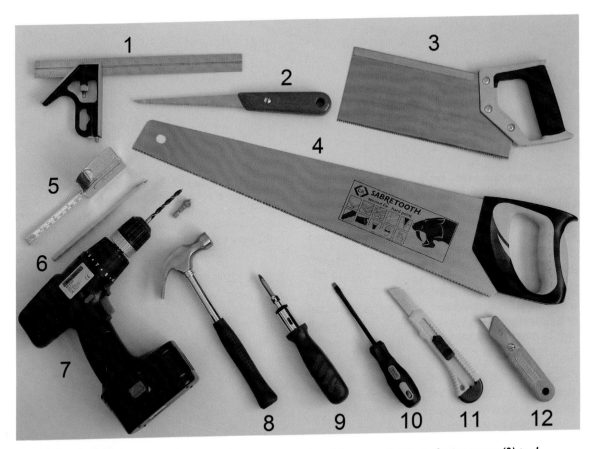

Fig. 11 *Construction tools for the folding box, baseboard and framework: (1) steel set-square; (2) pad saw; (3) tenon saw; (4) cross-cut saw; (5) steel tape-measure; (6) pencil; (7) cordless drill with drill bits and countersink; (8) hammer; (9) ratchet screwdriver with standard and cross-head attachments; (10) standard screwdriver; (11) craft knife with extending blade; (12) heavy-duty craft knife.*

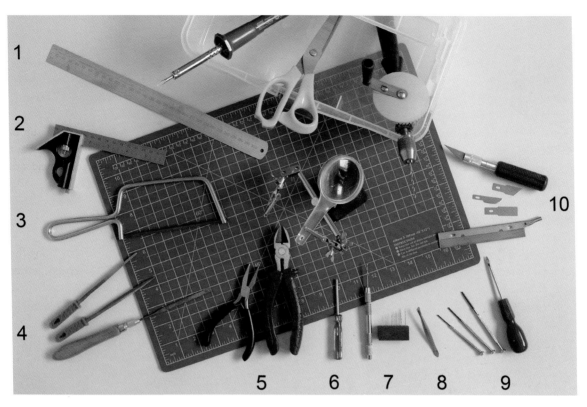

Fig. 12   Tools for modelling the layout: (1) steel rule; (2) small steel set-square; (3) small hacksaw; (4) assorted needle files and a rasp, not shown; (5) pliers for holding items and cutting wire; (6) bradawl; (7) pin vice with fine drills; (8) tweezers; (9) selection of small screwdrivers. (10) multi-purpose craft knife with various blades and razor saw attachment. Also shown are a general purpose soldering iron, scissors, small hand-drill and a 'helping hands' type of holding clamp with optional magnifying glass.

with the plywood folding box, consist of an HB-grade pencil, 3m (10ft) steel tape and a standard-size adjustable steel set-square. For cutting the timber framework for the base, a cross-cut or tenon saw is suitable. The tenon saw will provide a finer cut than the cross-cut saw, although plywood is easier to cut with a cross-cut saw. A pad saw is useful for cutting out the openings in the plywood sides of the layout to gain access to track running under the hills. Drilling holes for screws is accomplished with a cordless drill and a selection of drill bits for different screw sizes. Using a countersink bit will ensure screw heads sit flush with surfaces. Screwdrivers, such as a ratchet-type that takes both standard slot and cross-head bits, are handy for tight spaces, as is

a standard screwdriver for screws and opening tins of paint, etc. Finally, also useful are a small hammer for tapping in pins, a knife for removing burrs and trimming, and an extendable flexible-blade knife for cutting foam. These last three tools are also used for modelling the layout, in pinning track to the base, general cutting work and shaping the foam landscaping.

MODELLING TOOLS

The tools described here are suitable for the majority of model train layouts, including Teignside Quay. I suggest the first item to include in your tool armoury is a self-sealing, rubber cutting mat on which to conduct your cutting, gluing, painting and construction of items prior to placing them on your layout. Mats are available in various sizes and are helpfully marked in cm and 1in squares to assist in aligning walls when constructing buildings, for example. For measuring and also making straight cuts in sheet material, such as cork card and plastic, a steel rule for guiding the cut is used in conjunction with a craft knife. It is suggested that investment in a good-quality craft knife that accepts various shaped interchangeable readily available cutting blades, including a razor-saw attachment, should provide years of service. A steel set-square, smaller than its bigger brother used for constructing the folding layout, will assist in aligning items square and upright, such as in assembling kits of buildings and ensuring that tunnel entrances are vertical when fixing them to the base of the layout. Constructing items that involve cutting sheet metal and lengths of piano wire for making pulley shafts for working features, for example, will require a small hacksaw, a set of needle files, including a rasp for shaping foam, and pliers for holding objects and for cutting electrical wiring. For making very small holes in objects, such as for wiring and for fibre optics to pass through, a pin vice with a set of micro-size drill bits is suitable, together with a hand drill with a set of medium-size drill bits, and also a bradawl for making larger holes in softer materials. A selection of watchmaker-type screwdrivers, as well as tweezers for holding small items, is very useful. Household scissors are ideal for cutting card and even thin aluminium and brass sheets, although it is probably wise to buy scissors especially for your tool box rather than raiding the kitchen drawer.

Electrical wiring can be joined to miniature bulbs for lighting buildings; for example, with screw-type connecting blocks. However, there will be occasions where it may be necessary to solder wiring to electrical components and, therefore, a general purpose soldering iron is required. Although not essential, a 'helping hands' type of free-standing clamp, comprising of two adjustable articulated mounted crocodile clips with optional magnifying glass, is handy for holding small items for soldering or painting figures.

ADHESIVES

The range and diversity of adhesives, or glues for short, that are available to the modeller is considerable and probably more than is required for building the average layout. The majority of adhesives are toxic and some can give off fumes, so reading the manufacturers' labels before use is a priority. They must also be used in a well-ventilated area and stored securely away out of reach of children and pets. I describe here the main types of adhesives in common use together with their applications.

BALSA CEMENT

This is one of those traditionally used glues that has stood the test of time for joining balsawood together in constructing model flying aircraft and is equally suitable in making buildings and other structures from balsawood and card for model railways. It will dry in about 10 minutes and set hard within 12 hours. It should be applied sparingly though, as the cement tends to shrink on drying, which can distort card.

BLU-TACK

Although not a glue, Blu-Tack is useful for holding N-gauge vehicles, enabling them to be repositioned on roads. It is also useful for securing electrical wiring to the underside of the baseboard.

CONTACT ADHESIVE

This is available in two main strengths: medium strength for card and general craft applications, and heavy-duty strength for fixing tabletop laminates and heavier items. The medium-strength adhesive is adequate for model railways and is suitable for attaching figures and buildings to the layout. It will bond together most sheet materials; however, it can distort some of the thinner plastic sheets and may erode rigid foam if the adhesive is solvent-based, and it is therefore advisable to test on scrap material first. Normally the adhesive is smeared to both surfaces of the objects to be joined and left for around 5 minutes before bringing the surfaces together. The bond will set hard within 24 hours.

CYANOACRYLATE (SUPERGLUE)

This will bond together almost anything, including fingers if you are not careful! Stretching over the layout trying to extract a glue-smeared digit from part of the landscape with a razor blade is not to be recommended. The glue is almost instant-setting and works best for attaching small parts. A less instant-setting gel form of superglue is also available, enabling time to position parts. The glue makes an effective quick-drying sealant on small objects made from balsawood prior to painting. However, it is not suitable on rigid foam, as it will dissolve the material.

EPOXY ADHESIVE

Used for fabricating metal brackets and other parts on working features, for example. Metal to metal, metal to plastic or hard wood surfaces to be joined should be thoroughly scored with a file to provide a key for a physical, as well as a chemical, bond. It has excellent insulation qualities, making it ideal for use on electrical components. The adhesive comprises a resin glue and separate hardener, which is available in tube form or a syringe-type of dispenser. Setting times can vary between brands from 4 to 30 minutes, depending on what you require.

GLUE STICK

Commonly used in paper craft work and making greeting cards, it is also handy for quickly securing screwed-up paper on the layout for making foundations prior to laminating paper hills and raised verges. It comes in stick form in a lipstick-type dispenser – not to be confused, of course!

Fig. 13   The main types of adhesive for layout construction: (1) balsa cement; (2) Blu-Tack; (3) contact adhesive; (4) superglue; (5) epoxy adhesive – a plastic milk-bottle top is ideal for mixing together the resin and hardener; (6) twist-type glue stick dispenser; (7) low-tack glue; (8) liquid polystyrene adhesive and tube cement; (9) general purpose pva glue.

LOW-TACK GLUE

This is a rubbery compound that dries tacky, used for attaching coloured sponge foliage to tree armatures and for mounting bushes, also made from sponge, to the landscape.

POLYSTYRENE ADHESIVE

Also known as plastic cement, it is supplied in tube and liquid form. It has long been used for assembling plastic model aircraft kits and is equally suitable for assembling plastic kits of buildings, rolling stock and locomotives. It will bond together kits of buildings and other plastic structures, and also where these are constructed from raw materials, known as 'scratch building', using styrene sheet for the basic material. In tube form, one edge of the plastic item to be joined is coated with a thin layer of cement and the parts brought together. In liquid form, it is mostly supplied in bottles with sometimes a brush applicator in the lid. The parts are held together and the liquid is brushed along the joint, sealing the joint by capillary action. Both types of adhesive are solvents and work by dissolving the surface of plastic. Assembled parts can be handled within a few minutes and become fully hard in approximately 12 hours.

POLYVINYL ACETATE

More commonly known as white pva glue, this versatile glue will join most materials together. A multi-purpose pva glue is recommended for model railways. When used neat, it is suitable for wood, card, cork, paper, sponge and foam. Diluted with water, it is used for fixing ballast between rails, sealing porous filler, laminating hill surfaces with strips of paper and fixing scattered scenic grass and foliage to the landscape. It is recommended to apply it neat for fixing items such as trees, fences, telegraph poles and street-light columns. It dries in about an hour and will set in 24 hours, although it may take up to 48 hours to fully set when used on rigid foam. It does, however, have the advantage that the glue remains slightly flexible when set, allowing small movement in the joints of glued items that otherwise might break if accidently knocked.

Adhesives that boast 'All Purpose' on the label I find are generally OK for most materials but the solvent-based glues may not be suitable on some plastics and foam, so testing on scrap material first is advisable. Specialist adhesives are also available for card, foam and scenic material, including hot glue guns for general fixing of larger scenic items. Even hairsprays will fix scatter grass and foliage, providing a somewhat uncharacteristic sweet-scented perfume to your layout. The majority of these adhesives, such as pva, Blu-Tack, contact glue, epoxy resin, glue sticks and superglue, are generally available from hardware and DIY superstores, while hobby outlets will usually also stock these plus balsa cement, low-tack glue and polystyrene adhesive.

CHAPTER THREE

MATERIALS AND TECHNIQUES

Most of the materials listed here have been employed in constructing the folding layout Teignside Quay and this suggests that they are also suitable for constructing the majority of other types of fixed and portable layouts. For ease of reference, the materials are listed alphabetically and their uses described, as well as the techniques required.

ALUMINIUM SHEET AND TUBE

Perhaps not generally associated with the construction of model railways, but where working features are to be included on the layout, this material is useful in fabricating mountings for electric motors, brackets for pulley or gear axles, and protective shielding on electrical components, such as plug sockets. The tube form of the material is ideal for constructing columns for working street lighting and also piano-wire linkage guide tubing for remote working of manually operated turnouts.

The thinner aluminium sheets can be bent by hand, with pliers or in a vice. Being a soft material, it is easily cut with a hacksaw or heavy-duty scissors. Holes are best drilled slowly with a hand or power drill and edges smoothed with a file. Self-tapping screws will fasten metal to metal and timber screws will fasten wood. Epoxy, contact and superglue will also stick aluminium together and to wood after the surfaces of aluminium sheet are first roughed up with a file to provide a key.

BALSAWOOD

This has always been a popular modelling material owing to its combined strength, light weight and ease with which it can be cut with a knife or razor saw, and also shaped. It is available in standard lengths of 91cm (36in) in various thicknesses, also in block form and in handy packs of assorted sizes. Balsawood is suitable for stiffening card and

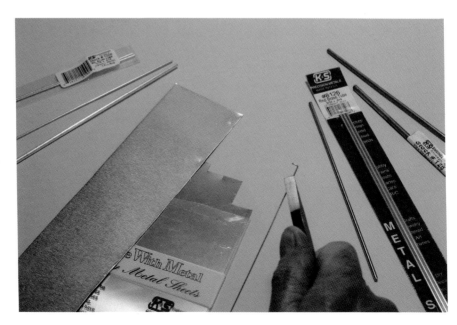

Fig. 14 The thinner sheets of aluminium and brass are available in handy packs and can be cut with heavy-duty scissors and bent with pliers or in a vice. Manually, remotely operated turnout linkages are made from piano wire and working street lighting from aluminium tube.

constructing buildings, bridges and other structures from scratch. Where a balsawood structure requires painting, apply two or three coats of cellulose dope or sanding sealer to seal the grain and lightly rub down with sandpaper between each coat before finishing with a top coat of paint to the required colour. On small items that require painting, the wood grain can be sealed by applying either balsa cement or superglue to the surface.

BRASS SHEET AND TUBE

The sheet form, when cut into strips, will make springy electrical wiper arms to provide switching or electrical current to moving parts in working railway features. Both the sheet and tube forms of the material will accept soldered electrical wiring connections. Axle shafts and bearings in working features are cut from brass tubes. Brass sheet can be cut, bent and glued using the same techniques as working with aluminium sheet.

CARD

My first introduction to card hailed from a time when coloured printed cowboy scenes were to be found on the back of a certain well-known cereal packet; these could be cut out to make some kind of rather wobbly ranch building. In recent years, card has suffered a decline in popularity as a construction material, due mainly to replacements such as plastic card (styrene sheet), which does not easily distort and can be painted with minimal preparation. Card does, however, still have a place for the railway modeller in making contoured formers in the construction of scenic hills, road bases and mock-ups of buildings, for example. A few manufacturers produce printed card kits of buildings in various scales, and with card being relatively lightweight, this makes it suitable for portable layouts. For making finished items, such as buildings from scratch or for use in the construction of roads, I suggest art-card or paper-faced mounting board is used due to their superior surface finish for painting on. Card is cut with a knife and will accept most

types of adhesives; clear-setting contact glue is particularly suitable as any surplus glue can, when dry, be easily rolled off with your finger without spoiling the adjoining surface of the card.

CORK

Available in sheet and strip form in 1.6mm ($\frac{1}{16}$in) and 3mm ($\frac{1}{8}$in) thickness, cork is normally sandwiched between the track and a composite fibre baseboard to aid silent running of locomotives and rolling stock. The strip form of cork is useful for supporting the track in tunnels to match the height of the ballasted track underlay of the remaining visible track on the layout. Cork can be cut with a knife and will accept pins for fastening the track, or contact glue is also suitable. Pva glue is used to fix cork to a foam baseboard. Strips of cork bark are also available in packs for representing realistic-looking rock faces on the landscape and, being featherweight, it is ideal for portable layouts. It is clean to use and easily shaped with a knife for gluing to the sides of paper-laminated hills, using either pva or contact adhesive.

RIGID FOAM

For the baseboard on Teignside Quay I used 19mm ($\frac{3}{4}$in) Styrofoam. This is a blue, rigid, cell foam more commonly used as insulation in the building trade but it is also available for general craft applications from craft and hobby suppliers in various sizes. The main advantage of using this material for the railway modeller is that it is extremely lightweight and can easily be cut and shaped with a knife. Using the hot wire method will also cut foam; however, this will generate toxic fumes, so this should only be done in a well-ventilated area. As with any layout, the base must be rigid and using foam is no exception; therefore, the foam base must be adequately supported on a timber frame to prevent warping or flexing. The only downside of foam is that it reacts with solvent-based adhesives, including superglue and some paints, which dissolve the foam. Also, the material being fairly soft, it is susceptible to fingernail digs. However, these minor niggles are overcome by

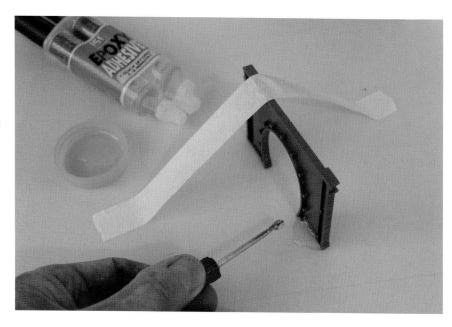

Fig. 15 Epoxy resin or solvent-free contact glue will fix plastic items, such as this Peco tunnel entrance, to Styrofoam. Masking tape supports the tunnel entrance upright until the resin or the glue has set.

fixing items with pva, solvent-free contact adhesive or epoxy glue. Painting exposed parts of foam, such as the underside of the layout, with two coats of household emulsion paint will help in providing a protective skin and in minimizing potential knocks and dents. As an aside, solvent-based contact glue, if applied thinly, will fasten items to emulsion-painted foam. To assist adhesion when laminating layers of Styrofoam together for building up landscaping, for example, scuff the slight surface sheen on the foam with medium grit glasspaper prior to applying neat pva glue. Once the laminated foam is glued together, either pin or hold it down with a weighted object until the glue has set. Setting time will be up to 48 hours but this may be reduced by applying gentle heat.

Pva glue is not very effective in securing edges, such as the narrow bases of plastic tunnel entrances, directly to the surface of the foam and, therefore, these items are glued with either epoxy or solvent-free contact adhesive. However, pva glue is suitable for securing plastic fence posts, trees and street-light columns by gluing these items into pre-made holes in the foam. Electrically operated turnout motors, which are either mounted directly under the foam baseboard or remotely operated on the surface via a wire linkage, are fastened with self-tapping screws directly into the foam by first applying pva glue to the tip of the screws and gently screwing them into the foam with just finger pressure. Once the glue has set, the turnout motor will be sufficiently secure for the normal operation of points. If for any reason the turnout motor requires removal, the screws are removed with a screwdriver in the normal way, thus breaking the glue bond with the foam.

Fig. 16 Applying pva glue to the tip of screw fastenings will secure points (turnout motors) to Styrofoam.

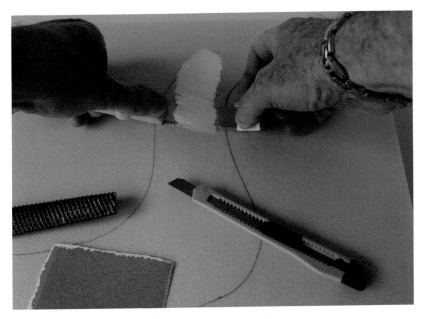

Fig. 17 For carving out concave areas in Styrofoam, such as a riverbed, an extending snap-off-blade type of knife is utilized by holding the extended blade in a curve and working it in a cutting and slicing action, taking care not to over-bend the blade. Masking tape is wrapped around the pointed blade end to protect fingers. Also shown here to aid shaping and carving foam are a woodworkers' rasp, coarse grit sandpaper and a smaller version of the extending blade knife.

Fig. 18 For finishing and getting into tight corners, this small handmade tool for carving foam consists of a razor blade, broken in half, curved and superglued into saw-cut slots in a hardwood handle.

Fig. 19 Using the razor-blade carving tool in the final stages of carving out a riverbed prior to smoothing with coarse grit glasspaper.

PIANO WIRE

This is available in standard 91cm (36in) lengths from model shops, and comes in various gauges (termed g. or swg.) from approximately 21g. (1/32in) up to 10g. (1/8in) diameter, which incidentally is the same diameter as Meccano axle shafts and will, therefore, accept Meccano, or equivalent, gears and pulleys for use in constructing working features. The thinner gauge wires can be soldered, superglued, or epoxy glued, and are suitable for making linkages for turnouts and signals. These thinner wires are cut and bent with pliers, whilst the thicker sizes are cut with a hacksaw and bent with the application of heat over a gas ring.

PLASTIC CARD

Also sometimes referred to as styrene sheet, this is available in about A4-size sheets in usually white or black of various thicknesses from 0.25mm (0.010in) to 2.0mm (0.080in). Embossed plastic card sheets of brickwork, stone, roof and slate tiles are

Figs 20 and 21   To cut plastic card, score the surface with a knife against a straight edge, such as a steel rule, then snap away the part required from the remaining sheet. For cutting ordinary card and sheet balsa, apply several light cutting strokes with the knife until the material is cut through. A razor saw is used for cutting through thicker sheets of balsa wood.

also available, including a strip form of the material for making fencing and buildings from scratch. The material can be drilled with a hand drill, filed, sanded, sawn with a razor saw or the thinner sheets cut with scissors. Most sheet material, such as balsa and card, is usually cut with a knife against a metal straight edge, such as a steel rule. However, when cutting plastic card with a knife, score the outline of the part required two or three times with a knife and bend away the surrounding sheet and the part will snap away. The thicker sheets of plastic card have limited bending ability and will easily snap. However, permanent bends can be made by pre-bending sheets in hot water first. Styrene solvent or plastic cement is used for gluing the material. The only preparation required for painting is to wash the item with mild detergent and then rinse to remove any grease prior to applying acrylic or enamel paint of the required colour. Windows for buildings can be made from the clear form of the material, or from clear acetate sheet, which is superglued or fixed with contact adhesive to the inside of the building.

SCENIC GRASS

Basically there are two types of scenic grass offered by manufacturers: grass mat and grass scatter.

GRASS MAT

This is available in rolls and also roughly A3-size mats in various shades of grass, which are cut to shape and contoured when applying to hills on larger layouts or where expansive areas of grass are required. Pva glue is brushed on to the surfaces to be covered and the mat is laid on top and held with pins, if necessary, until the glue has set.

GRASS SCATTER

Obtainable in packets of various shades of grass, in fine, medium, coarse and blended varieties. As with grass mats, the surfaces to be covered are first

Fig. 22   Examples of a cut section of grass mat and scatter-grass material produced by Woodland Scenics.

Fig. 23   Sprinkling grass-scatter material on a pva glue-coated section of verge. Excess grass scatter is vacuumed away once the glue has dried.

coated with pva glue and the scatter grass sprinkled on top with your fingers. Once set, excess scatter material is vacuumed away and further scatter grass of a different shade and texture can be added on top to provide different effects. Grass scatter is particularly useful where sharp hill contours require covering.

SOFTWOOD AND PLYWOOD

SOFTWOOD

This is the choice of timber for constructing the framework upon which the baseboard of a layout is supported, be it fibreboard or a foam base. Typically, 50 × 25mm (2 × 1in) planed timber is used, which is readily available from DIY superstores and timber merchants. When selecting softwood, check the timber is warp-free and does not have too many knots. Being a soft wood it is fairly easy to work with general woodworking tools, such as those shown in Chapter 2. Pva adhesive combined with woodscrews provide strong joints to the frame assembly.

PLYWOOD

Plywood is used for constructing the enclosure (carcass) of a portable layout in order to protect the layout within, and also for making removable panels for the backscene and to protect wiring under the baseboard. Plywood sheets are readily available in around 6mm (¼in) and 3mm (⅛in) thickness, which is suitable for constructing an enclosure of a medium- to large-size portable layout using general woodworking tools.

WATER FEATURE RESIN

This is a clear-setting resin for creating puddles, ponds, rivers and sea features. Several types of resin products are available on the market, such as a two-part application comprising a resin with separate hardener, and a hot-melt granular resin product. However, for ease of application I have found 'the straight from the bottle' type of resin gives realistic results. The resin is poured straight from the bottle into a shallow hollow to make a pond, for example, to a depth of about 3mm (⅛in), after first sealing and painting the bottom of the hollow with a muddy brown colour. A gel form of resin is also available for forming ripples, waves and waterfalls. Both resin types set in about 24 hours but may take longer when creating deeper water features.

MISCELLANEOUS MATERIALS AND ITEMS

This category includes additional items required for the main construction of Teignside Quay; other bits and pieces required, such as paint, screws, track accessories and electrical components, are described in the following chapters.

COPPER WIRE

Useful for creating armatures in forming contours to provide a foundation for paper-laminated surfaces in the construction of hills. Copper wire of around 1mm diameter is easily bent by hand and can be sourced from household heavy-duty electrical earth wiring obtained from electrical suppliers, and stripping away the plastic insulation from the wire.

FILLER

Cellulose or acrylic filler can be moulded into rock formations and realistic-looking rock shapes, and carved with a knife before the filler fully sets. Filler is always a must-have item for general gap-filling on the landscape and buildings, etc.

KITCHEN TOWEL

Apart from performing mopping-up duties, strips of kitchen towel can be laminated in layers with pva glue to form shell-like surfaces in the construction of hills and embankments.

Fig. 24   Clear, cold, curing resin and gel produced by Woodland Scenics for making water features are applied straight from the bottle.

Fig. 25   To make a wildlife pond simply compress Styrofoam to a depth of 3mm with your fingers to the required shape of your pond, as shown here in the foreground. Seal the compressed surface with pva glue and use acrylic paint to colour the bottom of the pond muddy brown; when dry, carefully pour in the clear resin making sure the Styrofoam base is level, otherwise you may have accidentally modelled a mini-Tsunami. Once the resin has set, finish off with scatter grass and undergrowth around the edge as shown part completed in the background.

MASKING TAPE

A versatile sticky tape that not only masks off unwanted areas from paint and for holding items, but is also useful in protecting trackwork when gluing scenic scatter grass to track verges and adjacent embankments. It is also used for webbing in the construction of hills.

CORDLESS HANDHELD VACUUM CLEANER

Last but certainly not least, this invaluable little helper is a necessity in removing construction debris within the layout, including excess scenic scatter grass, which can then be reused. For reaching awkward areas, I found it helpful to tape a length of plastic tube of about 5mm diameter on to the end of one of the cleaner attachments.

Fig. 26   *The basic hill structure showing copper-wire armatures and masking-tape webbing on to which strips of kitchen towel are laminated to form the hill surface.*

CHAPTER FOUR

CONSTRUCTING THE FOLDING LAYOUT

WHERE TO BUILD

This obviously depends on personal circumstances and, unlike a permanent layout where the choice of location can be a limiting factor, a portable layout, by definition, does not suffer from these constraints. Indeed, a small, portable, model train layout can quite easily be constructed at the kitchen table or on a work surface, where there are usually ample electrical sockets for plugging in power tools and extra lighting. All that is required is a suitable-size building board, made from plywood or similar material, on which to construct the layout and space to place tools. At the end of a building session, the board, together with the tools and construction materials, is simply stored away until next time.

For building a larger portable layout, it is preferable to allocate a specific space where this can be constructed without the necessity of having to clear everything away between day-to-day domestic duties. The main requirement is that the chosen location should have a large enough flat, level surface on which to position and assemble the timber frame of the layout. As a rough guide, a working space of at least 1m (approx. 3ft) wide is required around the outside of the layout when opened out flat. However, if space is at a premium, slide the layout up against a wall and just work on one side at a time. Other suggested locations of where to build are: loft, garage, shed, spare room and outside.

LOFT

Unfortunately, not all loft spaces are suitable for constructing a model railway. Many loft spaces in newer properties are cluttered with supporting roof trusses, although it may still be possible to utilize the space between the roof trusses, once suitable floor boarding is laid. This is best secured in place with screws to allow access to house wiring and pipework. It should be noted at the outset that any structural alterations should not be contemplated without first seeking professional advice and engaging the services of a qualified electrician for fitting power sockets and extra lighting. Importantly, you will need to check that the existing floor joists in the loft are strong enough to bear additional weight, which may require strengthening. One or two of the more useful alterations that you may wish to consider, apart from insulating under the roof, are installing Velux windows and enlarging the hatch access. Having to lop off chunks of your newly completed prize layout with a saw in order to get it out through the existing hatch space could be somewhat disheartening to say the least. Minor alterations to a loft, including installing electricity and floorboards, do not normally require planning permission. However, it is still advisable to check with your local planning authority of your intentions before proceeding with any work. If your property is rented, then you most certainly will require the permission of your landlord or property association before any structural alterations are contemplated.

GARAGE

Although garages were mostly originally intended to house the family car, in my experience the majority of garages nowadays seem to be used for anything but the car, which is either relegated to the driveway or just parked in the road. A garage that has a flat, concrete floor with power points and lighting is very suitable for the construction of a model railway. It may be helpful though to seal the concrete floor with a sealing paint to reduce dust, making the floor easier to clean. Also, painting the inside walls white will enhance the available lighting levels.

SHED

A purpose-built shed may be a luxury but an existing shed can quite easily be converted if it is in reasonable condition. However, check with your local planning authority if you are considering a new shed, particularly as to the size and its proposed location. The electrical supply for power points and lighting will require routing from the residual current device (RCD) consumer unit in your property, outside of your shed. If you have an old-style fuse-box unit in your property, then for safety you will require an RCD unit fitted in your shed. As already stated, this work should only be done by, or at least advice sought from, a qualified electrician.

SPARE ROOM

For me, this is my location of choice, as all the creature comforts of home are to hand – heating for those long, cold winter evenings and the room already fitted with adequate power points. Although, admittedly, I do use the garage for general woodworking, and indeed this is where the timber framework and carcass for Teignside Quay was constructed. If you live in a flat with no access to a loft or a shed, then a spare room, if available, may be suitable. However, I suggest before you eagerly start sawing and gluing pieces of timber together, that you take time either to remove the fitted carpet, if one is fitted, or protect it by laying sheets of hardboard loosely over the top.

OUTSIDE

What can be more pleasant than sawing and assembling the timber framework for a model railway outside on a summer's day? Any suitable, flat surface area, such as a patio or driveway, is all that is required, and perhaps a cooling glass or two of something refreshing. For using a drill off the mains,

*Fig. 27   **The author in the corner of the spare room pretending to look busy painting track rails. Good lighting and a comfortable adjustable chair contribute to an enjoyable modelling experience.***

Fig. 28 A multi-socket extension lead allows extra lighting and tools, etc., to be plugged in within arms' reach. This example also supports a telephone landline socket with power surge protection. Note the plug-in RCD socket adapter for using mains powered tools outside with an extension lead.

an extension lead plugged into an RCD socket adapter will be necessary, if you have an old-style fuse-box in your property.

CONSTRUCTING THE FOLDING LAYOUT

The framework for the base for Teignside Quay, and indeed for any sizeable model railway for that matter, forms the foundation that supports the track. Any twisting or sagging can cause trains to derail and points to malfunction. It may be tempting to rush this initial stage of the layout construction in your enthusiasm to get the trains up and running, but extra care taken here will be time well spent. Pva wood glue is used throughout construction.

FRAMEWORK

Traditionally, the framework supporting the base of a layout is constructed from 2 × 1in timber. However, in order to reduce the weight of the layout, I have used slightly smaller-sized timber members, measuring 45 × 19mm (1¾ × ¾in). This reduced size does not impair the structural integrity of the layout, as the plywood carcass will provide additional strength. DIY superstores generally

stock ready-planed timber in the most commonly used sizes. However, if you have difficulty in obtaining the size required, a timber merchant should be able to help.

Mark with a pencil and set-square the lengths of the main frame members, consisting of the front, back, sides and middle lengthwise members, working to the measurements shown in Fig. 29. As the two frame halves of the layout are both identical, both frame half-member lengths are marked and cut at the same time.

Lay one half-frame member on a flat surface to ensure the frame remains straight and level during assembly. Position the corners of the frame with a set-square and mark and drill holes for the screws. All the frame members are butt-jointed and glued and screwed together with 38mm (1½in) countersunk woodscrews, using two woodscrews for each joint.

Glue the joints and screw together through the pre-drilled holes, which are countersunk to enable the screw-heads to sit flush with the timber surface.

As an aside, self-drilling, countersunk woodscrews are available that are designed to cut their way through timber as they are screwed in, but personally I prefer to pre-drill holes to ensure that

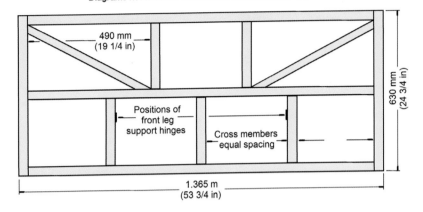

Frame halves constructed from 45 x 19 mm (1 3/4 x 3/4 in) timber

Diagrams not to scale. Construct to measurements only

490 mm
(19 1/4 in)

Positions of
front leg
support hinges

Cross members
equal spacing

630 mm
(24 3/4 in)

1.365 m
(53 3/4 in)

Fig. 29   Dimensions of the two identical frame halves for supporting the foam baseboard.

Fig. 30   Marking out the lengths of the timber-frame members in pairs using a set-square prior to cutting out with a saw. The workmate-type holding trestle, shown here, is ideal or an old table can be used for marking out and cutting timber.

Fig. 31   Mark the thickness of the frame as a guide to drilling holes for the frame-assembly screws, which are also countersunk using an electric drill or a hand countersinking tool.

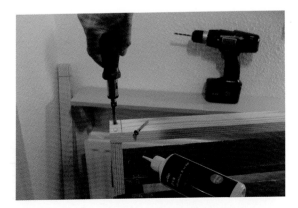

Fig. 32   Apply pva glue to the joints before the frame timbers are screwed together.

the screws are guided through the timber where they are intended, thus reducing the chances of the timber splitting.

To ensure the frame is held square during assembly, temporarily tack a batten or a spare frame member diagonally across two opposite corners and check the frame is square with a set-square. Repeat this assembly for the other half of the frame, which is constructed over the top of the first half to ensure that they match.

Mark with a set-square and cut to length the short cross-bracing members (five for each frame half). Three of the cross-bracing members are glued

Fig. 33   Lay each frame half on a flat surface, ensuring they are square, and temporarily tack a batten diagonally across opposite corners of the frame until the glued and screwed joints have set.

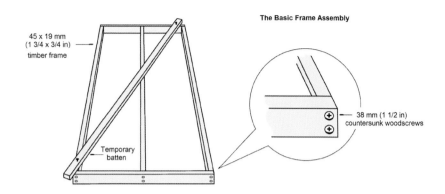

and screwed through pre-drilled holes, equally spaced between the back and middle lengthwise members on each frame half. The remaining two cross-bracing members are glued and screwed through pre-drilled holes on the other side of each half of the frame, between the front and middle lengthwise members.

Mark out and cut the diagonal members (two for each frame half), which are glued and screwed through pre-drilled holes at the outer corners of each frame half. The temporary diagonal holding batten can now be removed.

Fig. 34   Marking out the mitre joints and lengths of the four diagonal frame members by placing the members diagonally between the outer frame corners and cross-bracing members.

Fig. 35   Cutting one of the mitre joints and diagonal frame members to length. Shown in the background is a completed outer frame corner.

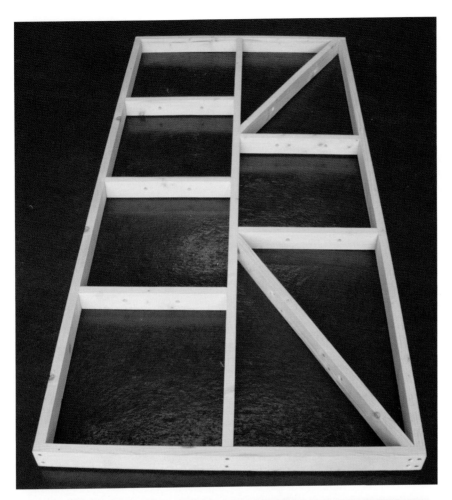

Fig. 36 One-half of the completed frame.

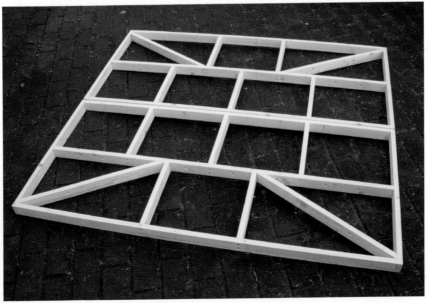

Fig. 37 Both frame halves temporarily placed together showing the overall frame layout. Holes are drilled at intervals through the frame members for electrical wiring to pass through.

TOP: **Fig. 38** *Pva glue is used to glue the foam base to the top of each frame half. The foam is held in place with strips of tape while the glue sets.*

BELOW: **Fig. 39** *Suggested arrangement for gluing smaller sheet sizes of foam to each frame half. Weights are used to hold the sheet foam in position.*

Joining Foam
For smaller sheet sizes of foam

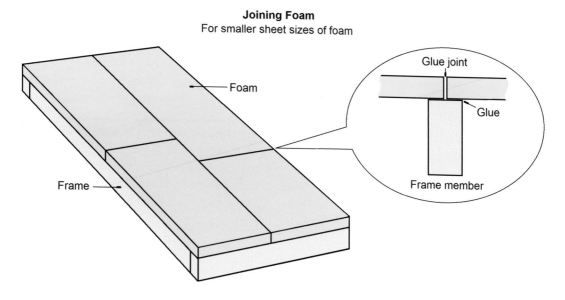

To allow for the routing of the electrical wiring for the track, points, lighting and working features to pass through, drill 10mm (⅜in) diameter holes midway along the inner frame members. Any protruding splinters around the holes should be smoothed flush, including any uneven frame joints, with glasspaper.

FOAM BASE

The base for the layout is cut from either 19mm (¾in) or 25mm (1in) Styrofoam. On Teignside Quay I used the 19mm thickness foam; however, if you have difficulty in obtaining this size, then the larger thickness of 25mm should not present any problems. Websites for suppliers of Styrofoam are listed at the back of this book. Overall sheet sizes of foam can vary between suppliers, and it may be the case that some suppliers do not stock the size of foam sheet required to cover all of each frame half in one go. However, this is not a problem as smaller sheet sizes can easily be butt-jointed together and the joints glued over an intermediate frame member.

Mark the outline of the foam base with a soft pencil, using each frame half as a template. Cut the base out with a sharp, long-blade knife and apply glue to all the upper surfaces of each frame half. Position the foam on top of the frames and hold in place with strips of masking tape until the glue has set. I suggest this should be for at least 48 hours to enable the glue to soak fully into the foam. Suitable weights are used to hold foam in place where the foam is butt-jointed over frame members. Finally, once the glue has set, sand the edges of the foam base flush with the frame sides.

BACK AND SIDES

The back and sloping side panels of the layout are constructed from 6mm (¼in) plywood and form an enclosed box arrangement when the layout is folded.

Working to the measurements shown in Fig. 40, draw on the plywood sheet the outline shape of one side panel only, using a straight edge and set-square to ensure that the corners with the base are square. Cut out the sloping side panel with a saw and smooth rough edges with glasspaper. Use this side panel as a template to draw the other sloping side panel on to the plywood sheet and cut out. Mark and cut square with the base the midway points on each side panel where the folding hinge will be located and smooth the edges.

Glue and screw the sloping side panels to the frame sides through pre-drilled holes using 12mm

(½in) countersunk woodscrews, noting that the base of the panels should protrude 6mm (¼in) at each end of each frame half.

The size of the plywood back panel is the same height as the back of the sloping side panels, and the length of the back panel is measured and cut to fit between them. Glue and screw the base of the back panel to the side of the rear frame using 12mm (½in) countersunk woodscrews through pre-drilled holes. The sides of the back panel are glued between the sloping side panels, and the corners where these meet strengthened with 30mm (1¼in) concave-shaped wood mouldings, glued on the inside of the corners. The concave shape of the mouldings also helps in smoothing out the inside corners on to which the backscene is painted.

To protect the edge of the Styrofoam base along the exposed hinge side of each frame half, and also the front edge of the frame, cut out three strips of 6mm (¼in) plywood to fit the width between the sloping side panels and to cover the depth of the edge of the exposed foam and frame sides. The plywood strips are screwed and glued to the frame sides through

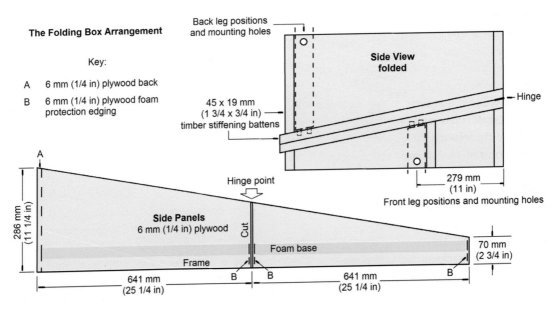

Fig. 40 Cut the side panels to the dimensions shown. The back panel is cut to the same height as the rear of the sloping sides, and the width of the panel cut to fit between the sides. Also shown for reference is the completed side-view arrangement.

pre-drilled holes using 12mm (½in) countersunk wood-screws.

To strengthen the ply-wood back and the sloping side panels, measure, cut, glue and screw 45 × 19mm (1¾ × ¾in) battens to the top outer edges, sides, corners and adjacent to the positions of the front leg mounting holes, using 12mm (½in) counter-sunk woodscrews through pre-drilled holes and smooth all edges flush with glass-paper.

TRAIN CONTROLLER POSITIONS

The layout is designed for either tabletop operation of trains with the train control-ler positioned on top of the baseboard, or with the layout mounted on legs and the option of positioning the train controller on a folding shelf arrangement underneath the baseboard. The train control-ler I used for Teignside Quay is quite a weighty item due to its integral mains trans-former, and therefore placing it directly on top of the rigid foam base would dent the surface. The solution to this was to stand the controller on a plywood platform, set into the foam base. This also provides a firm platform on which a panel with various switches for operating light-ing, working features and manually operated points can be mounted.

Fig. 41   Near completion of the back half of the layout carcass. The external stiffening battens and the plywood strip to protect the edge of the foam base have been fitted, together with the back panel concave corner mouldings. Part of one of the folding hinges has also been temporarily screwed in place.

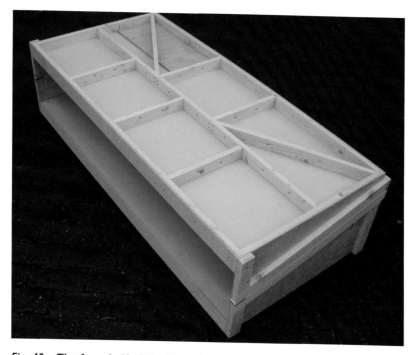

Fig. 42   The front half of the folded layout carcass, showing the remaining stiffening battens and plywood strip to protect the edge of the other half of the foam base. Note the position of the plywood train controller base.

Train Controller Platform

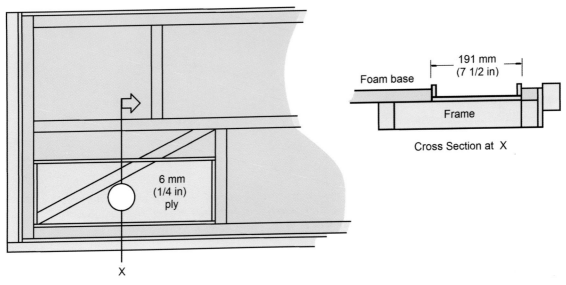

Fig. 43 *The train controller platform and sides are constructed from plywood and are glued into the bottom-left or the right-hand corner of the layout, if required. Note the large hole for the train controller mains lead and plug to pass through.*

Train Controller Baseboard Platform

Cut out a rectangular opening in the foam to the size and position shown in Fig. 43, using a straight edge and knife. The cut-out piece of foam is used as a template for marking on the outline for the plywood base, which is cut out using a saw from 6mm (¼in) plywood sheet.

MIDDLE LEFT: **Fig. 44** *Top view showing the completed plywood train controller platform, glued into the foam base of the front half of the layout.*

BOTTOM LEFT: **Fig. 45** *Underside view of the train controller platform, which here shows the platform slightly recessed within the diagonal frame member to allow the option of the controller unit to sit lower within the layout. Also shown is the back panel of the layout, whereby the panel is constructed in two halves and joined with a plywood pad, glued and tacked together, rather than using a single, large sheet of plywood for the panel. This option is useful when only smaller sheet sizes of plywood are available.*

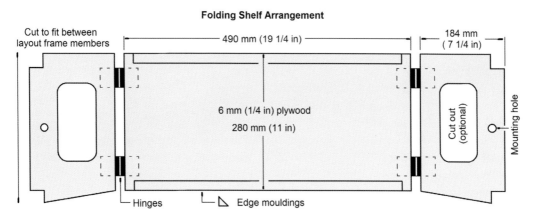

Folding Shelf Arrangement

Cut to fit between layout frame members

490 mm (19 1/4 in)

184 mm (7 1/4 in)

6 mm (1/4 in) plywood
280 mm (11 in)

Cut out (optional)

Mounting hole

Hinges

Edge mouldings

Fig. 46 *If you want the option of the folding shelf, mark on a plywood sheet the size and shape of the shelf and cut out. Please note, the distance across the tops of the shelf sides will require measuring to enable the shelf to be cut to fit between the underside of the frame members.*

Glue the plywood base on top of the now exposed part of the diagonal timber-frame member, ensuring it is level, and secure the base with panel pins. Cut out four strips of 6mm (¼in) plywood, measured to fit the exposed sides of the foam opening. These are glued to the sides of the foam opening and to the plywood base.

Train Controller Shelf Arrangement

The advantage with this option is that more space is made available for track and scenery. The shelf is fastened with small wing-nuts to the underside of the baseboard timber frame and is designed to fold flat for storage when not in use.

Mark out the shelf base and sides on to 6mm (¼in) plywood sheet, as shown in Fig. 46, and cut out using a saw. To strengthen the base and to stop small items from rolling off, cut two lengths of 10mm (⅜in) quadrant-shaped timber edge mouldings and glue and tack these to the front and back edges of the shelf.

Screw two small flap-type metal hinges to each of the folding sides and to the base, ensuring that the sides can be folded back flat against the shelf.

Fig. 47 *Flap-type hinges are screwed to the underside of the shelf for attaching the sides to, and also allow the sides to be folded back against the shelf for storage. To prevent the sides flapping about when the shelf is stored, and to provide stability when it is attached to the layout, the hinge pins are removed and replaced with a nut and bolt, thus allowing the hinges to be tensioned. The pins are removed by filing off the hinge pin heads.*

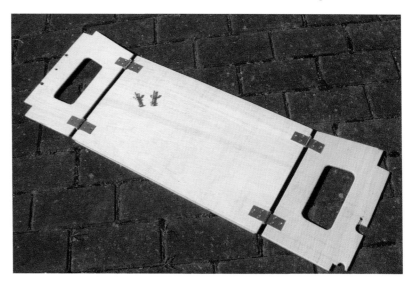

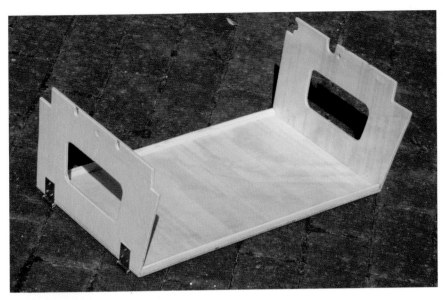

Fig. 48 The shelf, right side up, clearly shows the quadrant-shaped mouldings, which are glued and pinned to the front and back edges of the shelf. It may be necessary to cut one or two slots in the top of the sides to prevent obstructing electrical wiring when fastening the shelf in position under the completed layout.

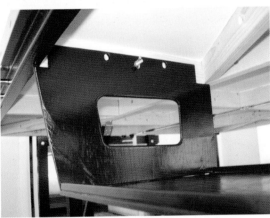

Fig. 49 The shelf is fastened to the layout with a small wing-nut and bolt through the folding sides of the shelf.

are removed and replaced with a nut and bolt. It is then a relatively simple matter to separate the two halves for transportation, and also it makes it easier to access areas for working on.

In order for the layout to close without a gap between the two halves of the layout, cut recesses

Fig. 50 To enable the two halves of the layout to be separated on completion, remove the hinge pins and replace with a nut and bolt, in a similar method to the shelf hinges. Recess each hinge to the depth of each hinge flap into the tops of the timber-strengthening battens, so that the layout closes without a gap. A tenon saw is used to cut the rebate for recessing the hinges, which are then screwed in place.

Measure and cut out the top corners of the sides to allow the shelf to fit snugly up against the under-side of the timber frame. Drill a hole in the top of the shelf sides to accept small wing-nut bolts with corresponding mounting holes drilled through the frame members.

THE LAYOUT HINGE JOINT

The two halves of the layout are hinged at the top of each of the sloping sides with flap-type metal hinges. To assist portability, the original hinge pins

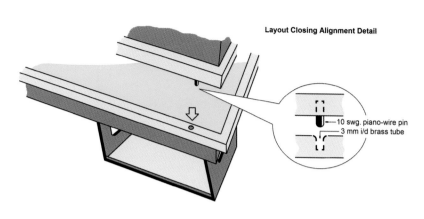

Fig. 51   This arrangement will ensure the layout closes in correct alignment. The tip of 10g. piano wire is rounded with a file and cut to make locating pins, while the brass tube is belled out at the top by using a hammer and a metal punch or steel rod. Both the piano-wire pins and brass tube are epoxy glued into pre-drilled holes. Also shown for reference is the location of the folding shelf unit.

Layout Closing Alignment Detail

10 swg. piano-wire pin
3 mm i/d brass tube

in the top of the sloping sides for the hinges to sit in and screw the hinges in place through pre-drilled holes with the countersunk woodscrews, usually supplied with the hinges.

To ensure the layout closes together in correct alignment, cut two short dowel pins from 10-gauge piano wire and round off the ends with a file. Epoxy glue the dowel pins into pre-drilled holes with 10mm (⅜in) protruding, one in each corner face of the back half of the layout, with corresponding short lengths of brass tubing, belled out and epoxy glued flush into pre-drilled holes in the corner faces of the front half of the layout. The layout should now fold together with the piano-wire dowel pins engaging with the brass tubing, thus preventing any sideways movement.

PROTECTION PANEL

With the layout closed for storage, the open hinged side is exposed to possible damage to track and scenery. To remedy this, a removable panel is made to cover this open area, and to make the panel more compact for storage, it can, if required, be constructed in two halves.

Trace the outline from the open hinged side of the closed layout on to 6mm (¼in) plywood sheet and cut out the panel with a saw. Measure the midway point, cut the panel in half and smooth the edges. However, another option is to cut the panel as one piece to cover the whole side of the layout;

the panel then can also double up as the painted backscene, which is adapted to slot in the back of the opened-out layout. (Details of this option are described in Chapter 7.)

Whichever option you decide upon, it is necessary to strengthen the panels to withstand the full weight of the completed, folded layout when it is standing on the floor. To strengthen the panels, cut 45 × 19mm (1¾ × ¾in) timber battens to length, and glue and screw the battens to the plywood panels, in the positions shown in Fig. 52, through pre-drilled holes using 12mm (½in) countersunk woodscrews. Note, if the panel is to be cut in half, the middle spanwise batten, which overlaps the panel joint, is glued and screwed to one panel half only.

To prevent any chance of the panels damaging the edges of the track and landscaping when the panels are fastened in place, glue 12mm (½in) wide strips of hardboard to the inside perimeter edges of each panel. The panels are required to have holes drilled through them to match the same hole positions for fastening the baseboard joint (see the section Securing the Baseboard Joint on page 44). The panels are fastened with the same coach bolts and wing-nuts used to fasten the legs when the legs are removed for storage. For additional security, small hook and eye (or screw) fastenings are fitted between the panels and layout frame after painting or varnishing the layout carcass.

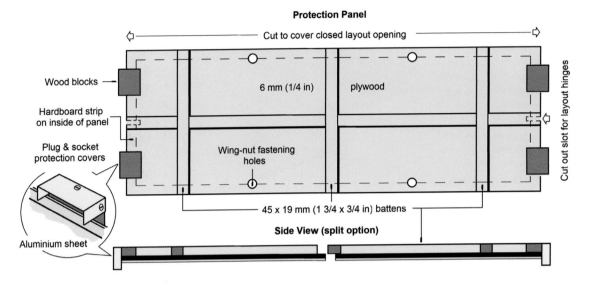

Protection Panel

Cut to cover closed layout opening

Wood blocks

6 mm (1/4 in) plywood

Hardboard strip on inside of panel

Plug & socket protection covers

Wing-nut fastening holes

Cut out slot for layout hinges

Aluminium sheet

45 x 19 mm (1 3/4 x 3/4 in) battens

Side View (split option)

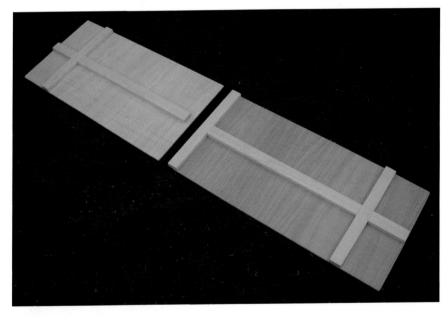

ABOVE: *Fig. 52 The protection panel can either be constructed as a single panel spanning the width of the closed layout, or constructed in two halves as shown in the side view. A slot is cut into each end of the panel so it fits flush over the hinge pivot bolts when the layout is closed.*

LEFT: *Fig. 53 Shown here is the completed 'split in half' version of the protection panel ready for varnishing.*

LEGS AND WHEELS

The option of removable legs allows freedom as to where the layout can be located, and also assists manoeuvrability on the floor; thus, 38mm (1½in) diameter castors are fitted on to the ends of the legs. This feature will be of benefit where working space may be restricted, whereby the layout can be just swivelled around to gain access to areas that might have otherwise have been difficult to reach.

Traditionally, legs or supports are constructed from 50 × 25mm (2 × 1in) timber, which is adequate for the majority of static layouts. However, we need to step up a gear here where castors are to be fitted, and, therefore, a slightly larger timber size is specified for the legs on Teignside Quay.

Working to the measurements shown in Fig.54, cut four legs from 64 × 38mm (2½ × 1½in) timber, noting the positions in Fig. 40 of the front and back

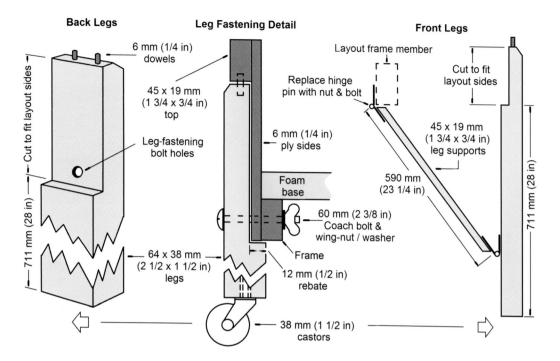

Back Legs

Cut to fit layout sides

711 mm (28 in)

Leg Fastening Detail

6 mm (1/4 in) dowels

45 x 19 mm (1 3/4 x 3/4 in) top

Leg-fastening bolt holes

64 x 38 mm (2 1/2 x 1 1/2 in) legs

6 mm (1/4 in) ply sides

Foam base

Frame

12 mm (1/2 in) rebate

38 mm (1 1/2 in) castors

Layout frame member

Replace hinge pin with nut & bolt

60 mm (2 3/8 in) Coach bolt & wing-nut / washer

Front Legs

Cut to fit layout sides

45 x 19 mm (1 3/4 x 3/4 in) leg supports

590 mm (23 1/4 in)

711 mm (28 in)

ABOVE: **Fig. 54** *Legs are constructed to the dimensions shown, and are fastened to the layout using wing-nuts and bolts. To add stability, wooden dowels are glued into the top of the legs, which locate into pre-drilled holes in the top of the layout sides.*

RIGHT: **Fig. 55** *A cross-cut saw is used to cut the 12mm rebate at the top of each leg, the height of the layout sides, and hardwood dowels glued into pre-drilled holes. The hole for the leg-fastening bolt has also been drilled together with a matching corresponding hole through the sides of the layout frame.*

legs on the sides of the carcass where the legs are fastened directly against the vertical stiffening battens. Measure the length of the rebated depth of the four legs where they fasten against the sides of the layout carcass and add this measurement to the length of the legs, as shown. Cut the legs to their overall length, noting that the top of the legs are cut to the same angle as the underside of the sloping stiffening battens on the carcass sides.

Holding the legs in position against the sides of the layout, mark on the inner side of the legs the extent of 12mm (½in) rebate and cut this out using a cross-cut saw.

Glue two 6mm (¼in) wood dowels into the top of each leg, leaving 10mm (⅜in) protruding, and drill corresponding holes where the dowels in the legs will engage into the undersides of the stiffening battens of the layout sides.

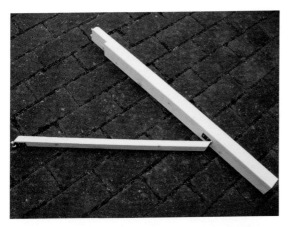

Fig. 56   *The diagonal front-leg bracing supports are fastened with hinges, screwed to the front legs. The position of the lower hinges is attained with the front legs bolted to the layout.*

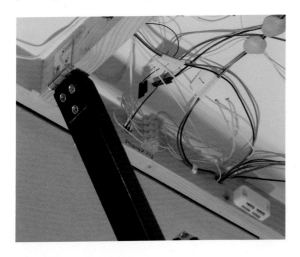

Fig. 57   *Position of one of the two upper, diagonal, front-leg bracing supports, fastened to the layout frame member with a hinge, the pin of which has been replaced with a nut and bolt to enable the legs to be removed for storage. One of the hardboard panel magnetic catches is also in view.*

The legs are fastened to the layout with 60mm (2⅜in) bolts and wing-nuts. Suitable holes for these are first marked and drilled through the legs. Using the holes in the legs as a guide, hold the legs in position and drill corresponding holes through the sides and frame of the carcass.

The front legs are each supported by a diagonal 45 × 19mm (1¾ × ¾in) timber bracing, which is measured and cut to length, as shown. Screw a flap-type hinge to both ends of each support bracing through pre-drilled holes. The hinge pins on the upper hinges (layout end) are replaced with a nut and bolt to allow removal of the legs for storing flat.

Bolt and wing-nut the front legs in place and diagonally position the support bracings between the legs and to the underside of one of the layout frame members. Screw the support bracing hinges to the legs and frame members through pre-drilled holes. The front legs can now be removed for storage by first removing the nuts and bolts in the upper support bracing hinges, attached to the layout frame, and then undoing the leg wing-nuts.

Castors are available with either a base-plate mounting, which is screwed into timber, or a pivot and socket type mounting that requires just a single hole to be drilled into timber to accommodate the castor pivot socket. For simplicity, the latter type of castor mounting is used here, fastened to the base of each leg.

SECURING THE BASEBOARD JOINT

The layout, in the opened-out position, is secured in place using two 60mm (2⅜in) coach bolts and wing-nuts. These are fastened through pre-drilled holes at the joint of the folding baseboard frame sections at a point 310mm (12¼in) from each side of the layout, as shown in Figs 58 and 59. Note the steel washer for making the electrical contacts between the two halves of the layout.

Ensure that the two baseboard sections, where they join together, are level and align correctly with each other. Any discrepancies here should be rectified at this stage by using a rasp and glasspaper, and checking levels with a straight edge.

Layout Joint-Fastening Arrangement

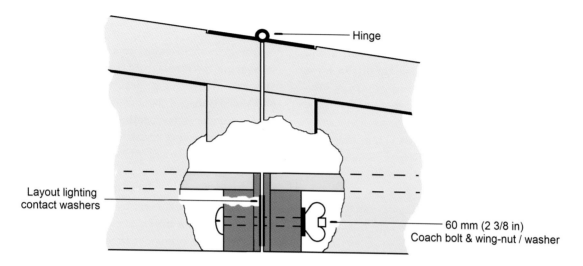

Hinge

Layout lighting
contact washers

60 mm (2 3/8 in)
Coach bolt & wing-nut / washer

Fig. 58 Cut-away view showing the layout secured in the open position. 25mm (1in) diameter steel washers are screwed to each frame to provide electrical contacts between the two halves of the layout.

Fig. 59 The steel contact washers are screwed in place through pre-drilled holes with countersunk woodscrews. Electrical connecting wires are attached at the wiring stage of the layout.

COVER UP

This should actually be the final part of the project, whereby removable hardboard panels are fitted to the underside of the layout to protect electrical wiring and the working mechanisms. However, in order to prevent potential damage to the wiring, etc., it may be prudent to fit the necessary panel-retaining guides and catches at this stage. It is only necessary for the panels to be removable where quick access may be required. For other areas under the layout, where there is minimal or no wiring, for example, panels can be screwed directly to the frame.

Measure and cut out eight panels from hardboard (four each side of the layout) and cut out openings for access to the leg and layout fastening bolts. It does not matter how the panels are configured, as this depends on where quick and easy access is required. However, the panels should be cut to a size so that all the edges are supported by a frame member.

One side of the removable panels are retained in position by slotting them under metal guides, as shown. The metal guides are made from 10mm (⅜in) wide L-shaped aluminium strip, cut into 50mm (2in) lengths to form each guide. The panel retaining guides are screwed equally spaced through pre-drilled holes in one side of the frame members, as shown. The other sides of the panels are retained in place with magnetic catches, screwed though pre-drilled holes in the corresponding frame side. To be able to release the panels, cut 25mm (1in) diameter finger-pull holes in the panels adjacent to the magnetic catches.

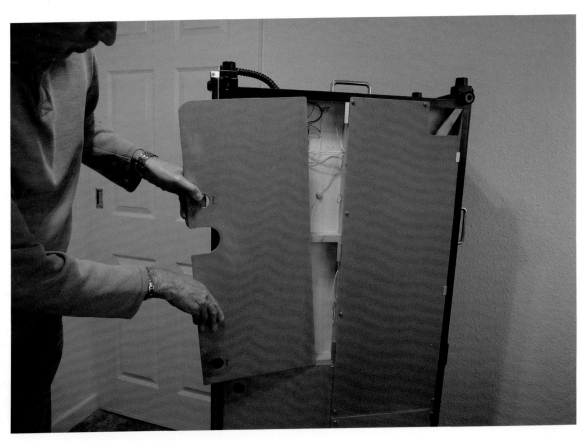

Fig. 60 Hardboard panels to protect electrical wiring under the layout are quickly removed courtesy of magnetic catches.

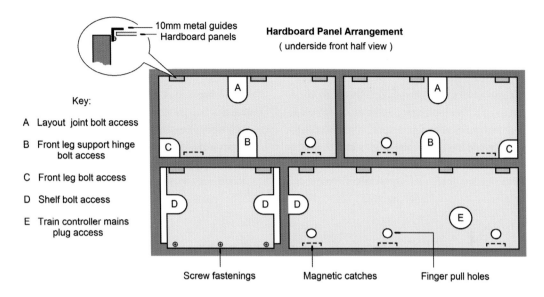

Fig. 61 The suggested arrangement for the hardboard panels on the front half of the layout to protect the wiring on the underside of the baseboard. For fastening the optional shelf, the smaller panel is cut to leave a gap on each side to accommodate the shelf sides. The same number and arrangement of panels for the back half of the layout have holes cut to access the back legs and the layout fastening bolts, similar to the front half of the layout. Fasten the panels to the layout frame with either roundhead woodscrews or magnetic catches.

Finally, smooth all the edges and round off corners using glasspaper. To protect and toughen the hardboard, apply two or three coats of pva glue to all edges and corners of the panels, including the access openings and finger-pull holes.

PAINT OR STAIN

Baseboard

To help provide a protective skin against nail digs and dents to the Styrofoam baseboard, apply two coats of household matt emulsion paint to the top surface and also underneath the baseboard. It is suggested a light colour is applied, such as white or light blue, to show up pencil marks when plotting on the track layout and positions of lineside items. The painted surface also provides a protective skin for attaching small items to the foam with thinly applied solvent-based contact glue, which might otherwise dissolve the foam if left unpainted. It is advisable to test first on a scrap piece of painted foam, as different makes of contact adhesive may react differently.

Carcass and Legs

The appearance of the plywood carcass of the layout, including the legs, will be enhanced by either painting it or applying a wood-stain varnish, which will also help to protect the wood against the occasional knock. Whatever type of finish you choose, it is easier and less messy to screw the catches and other fittings in place after the painting or varnishing is completed.

For the painting option, the carcass and legs will first require an undercoat, lightly rubbed down with fine-grade glasspaper, followed by two top coats of exterior-quality paint of the colour of your choice. The wood-stain varnish option is available in various shades and should preferably be of exterior-quality, which is applied directly to the timber. Two coats will generally be sufficient, again lightly sanded down between coats.

Fig. 62 *Three examples of paint and wood-stain varnish suitable for enhancing and protecting the layout. Household matt emulsion paint, as used on walls and ceilings, is painted on both sides of the foam baseboard to help protect the surface. For painting the carcass and legs, an undercoat and a couple of top coats of exterior-quality gloss paint will normally be required. For the option of a wood-stain pigmented varnish finish, two coats are applied direct to the timber. As with gloss paint, exterior-quality stained varnish is used. The surface finish of the painted or varnished options will benefit from a light sanding between coats when dry.*

FASTENINGS AND FITTINGS

The fastenings and fittings used during the course of constructing the layout are general household items that are readily available from hardware shops and DIY superstores. The remaining fittings required are lever-type catches, handles and, perhaps surprisingly, door-stops – all will be explained. These remaining fittings are shown in Fig. 64 and are fitted after the painting or varnishing is completed. Lever-type catches for securing the closed layout are fastened in place with small, round-head woodscrews. Metal handles for moving the layout around on its castors are bolted or screwed through the sides of the frame through pre-drilled holes. Door-stops are fitted to serve as feet, as

well as handholds, when lifting the layout. They also protect the plug and socket layout connections and provide the necessary ground clearance for the external fittings when the layout is placed on the floor. The door-stop feet/handholds are fitted as follows:

- Cut out eight 45mm (1¾in) square blocks from 19mm (¾in) timber and drill a 5mm (³⁄₁₆in) diameter hole through the centre of each block.
- Screw eight 19mm (¾in) high door-stops through the square blocks, one to each end corner of the layout using 38mm (1½in) woodscrews.
- The timber blocks can be painted or varnished, if required, to match the layout carcass.

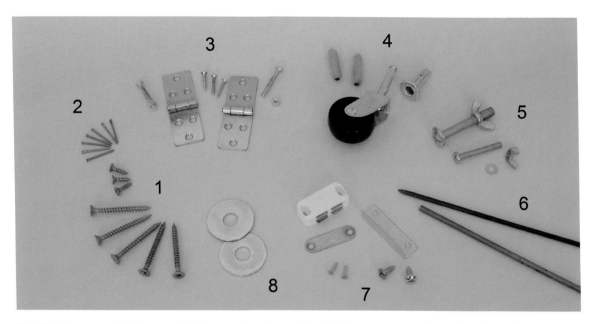

Fig. 63 Screws and fittings used during construction of the folding carcass are shown here for reference purposes: (1) the two main sizes of countersunk woodscrews used in the construction of the framework and the back and sides of the layout; (2) panel pins are useful for light assembly work such as in constructing the train controller platform; (3) ten back-flap hinges provide the folding joints for the layout, front-leg supports and the optional shelf arrangement, and small nuts and bolts are used to replace most of the hinge pins; (4) wood dowels and furniture castors for the legs; (5) six large wing-nut and bolts fasten the legs to the layout and secure the layout when opened out, while the two smaller sizes secure the optional shelf to the layout; (6) brass tube and piano wire form the correct alignment when closing the layout; (7) magnetic catches and metal guides, cut from aluminium angle section, for attaching the hardboard panels covering the layout wiring; (8) steel or brass washers are used for making electrical contacts between the two halves of the layout.

Fig. 64 After the carcass has been painted or varnished, the following fittings are attached: (1) four clasp-type catches to secure the closed layout; (2) seven metal handles to aid moving the opened layout about; (3) eight door-stops are screwed through timber blocks into each corner of the carcass sides to provide combined feet and hand-holds, while a further fourteen door-stops are screwed directly into the carcass and the protection panel to provide feet and to protect the remaining corners; (4) six hook-and-screw fasteners help to secure the protection panel to the layout, in addition to the same four wing-nut bolts that fasten the legs when they are not attached to the layout.

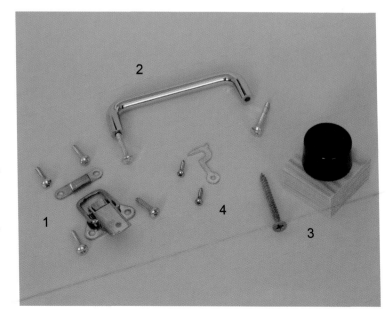

- Screw a further fourteen door-stops of the same height, directly to each of the remaining corners of the layout base, sides and the protection panels with 38mm (1½in) woodscrews.
- All the aforementioned items are screwed through pre-drilled holes in the layout.
- Only two door-stops are necessary on the back of the layout as the two metal handles also serve as feet.

There are a few other fittings, such as the plug-and-socket arrangement for connecting the electrical wiring between the two folding halves of the base-board, which are fitted during the wiring stage. Also, at the landscaping stage, the openings through the back and side of the layout to gain access to track under the hills are cut out and covered with small hinged plywood panels.

Figures 65–78 show the general arrangement of the completed carcass and the positions of fittings.

Fig. 65 *The protection panel fitted to cover the exposed hinged halves of the folded carcass to protect the layout when stored or transported.*

Fig. 66 *The four large wing-nut bolts that fasten the legs to the layout; also, when the legs are stored, secure the protection panel on the folded layout through the same holes, which accommodate the wing-nut bolts for fastening the two halves of the layout together when the layout is opened out.*

LEFT: *Fig. 67 One of the six hook-and-screw fastenings provide additional security in holding the protection panel to the layout.*

Fig. 68   Arrangement of the hardboard panels to protect the electrical wiring under the back half of the layout.

Fig. 69   Arrangement of the hardboard panels to protect the electrical wiring under the front half of the layout. Step-by-step instructions for assembling the layout are pasted on to the protection panel.

Fig. 71 Side view showing the four corner door-stop feet screwed through timber blocks to provide floor clearance for the layout catches and the electrical connecting plugs, which are stowed out of harm's way in holster-type covers, fabricated from aluminium sheet. This arrangement is repeated for the other side of the layout.

Fig. 70 General view of the back of the folded layout. The small, hinged panel covers access to the track running under one of the hills; this and the other access under the cable-car hill are cut out at the landscaping stage and plywood hinged covers are screwed to the back and side of the layout carcass.

RIGHT: Fig. 72 Locating one of the back legs into the side of the layout; the remaining legs are located in the same way.

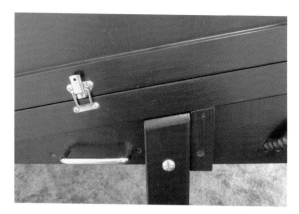

Fig. 73 Position of one of the front legs. Also shown is one of the lever-type catches to secure the layout when it is closed.

Fig. 74 Front-leg wing-nut bolt fastening. The remaining legs are fastened in the same manner to the sides of the layout. Also in view is one of the hardboard panel aluminium angle-retaining guides.

Fig. 75 Holes are cut into the hardboard panels for accessing the leg fastenings and the small hinge bolts that secure the front-leg supports.

Fig. 76 Metal guides are cut from L-shaped aluminium strip to hold one side of the removable hardboard panels that protect the wiring under the layout. The opposite side of the panels can either be fastened with magnetic catches or the panels screwed to the frame.

Fig. 77 The completed carcass standing on its legs ready to accommodate the start of laying the track.

Fig. 78 The optional shelf fastened in position, handy for holding railway items or for locating the train controller.

ASSEMBLY SEQUENCE

Now that the carcass is virtually completed, it is recommended that the assembly and dismantling sequence is rehearsed before starting on the business of laying the track and commencing the landscaping work. Trying to rectify any folding issues after the layout is completed could at best just be a minor inconvenience, or possibly having to undertake invasive surgery, such as modelling a bomb crater in one half of the folding layout into which to accommodate the tip of a church spire on the other half of the layout, as an extreme example. Therefore, with this in mind, please occasionally take time to check the clearance between the tops of the trees, hills and buildings with the layout folded as construction progresses.

The following suggested assembly sequence, which can be done by one or two people, where an extra pair of hands is helpful, applies to the completed layout, and includes fastening the optional shelf and legs, together with plugging in the train controller and electrical connections between the two halves of the baseboard.

Step 1

Position the layout on its side with the two halves of the protection panel uppermost, release the side hooks and remove the four wing-nut/bolts holding the panels (reuse these when fastening on the legs). Remove the two halves of the protection panel.

Step 2

Lower the layout so the larger half of the base is sitting on the floor and release the four side-clips holding the base halves together.

Step 3

Turn the layout on to its rear end and pull open from the bottom, and fully unfold on its hinges and fasten the layout halves together with two wing-nut/bolts through the holes at the baseboard joint.

Step 4

Wing-nut and bolt front legs in place and use a small nut and bolt to secure the leg supports through the hinge fastenings on the underside of the layout. Lower the layout to the floor and raise the back level to wing-nut and bolt rear legs in position.

Step 5

Unfold the optional shelf with the hinges facing outwards and secure to the underside of the front right-hand side of the layout using two small wing-nut/bolts through the frame members.

Step 6

Unfold the backscene panel and slot into the back of the layout.

Step 7

Plug together the baseboard wiring connectors at the side of the layout and the train controller, which is plugged into the multi-pin socket in the controller platform with the mains cable and plug passed through the large hole in the platform base.

To dismantle follow the above steps in reverse order.

CHAPTER FIVE

TRACKWORK AND WIRING

Now that the folding baseboard and carcass is completed, at last building the layout can commence. It may be that, rather than build the Teignside Quay layout design described here, you may wish to build a layout to your own freelance design or to replicate, in part, a scale version of a full-size railway, such as a station terminus or an industrial scene. Fortunately, the ample dimensions of the carcass do provide some versatility as to the choice of track gauge that can be accommodated, from the diminutive Z gauge up to OO gauge, whereby a circular track with perhaps a couple of sidings, including a passing loop, is feasible. Whatever your choice of track gauge, consideration has to be given at an early stage as to how your layout will be electrically operated in respect of choosing either digital command or analogue control, and whether to use insulfrog or electrofrog points.

I will admit that my initial design sketches for Teignside Quay were wildly overambitious, with impossibly tight curves and multiple sidings, in an attempt to cram as much track as possible within the layout. The lesson here is to keep it simple if you are designing your first layout, or to choose a published design that is within your modelling capabilities. The amount of time that you wish to spend on your layout may also be important to you, especially if you have a busy lifestyle. Generally speaking, the larger and more detailed the layout, the more time it will take to complete.

MARKING OUT

If you are designing your own track plan, the first step, after making the initial scale drawing on A3-size graph paper following the method suggested in the section Design Considerations in Chapter 1, is to mark on 305mm (12in) square grid, lines to the same scale as your drawing, starting at the bottom-left corner and then marking the same corresponding grid-lines full-size on to your layout. It is then just a matter of plotting full-size

Fig. 79 This relatively simple track plan for an OO-gauge run-around-type layout will sit comfortably within the folding carcass and would be suitable for short train formations rather than tail-chasers. To maximize track space, the train controller could sit on the shelf under the layout. The method of plotting the full-size track formations on to the layout from a scale drawing using the grid system can be applied to any gauge. Ensure grid lines are drawn accurately and are square on both your scale drawing and the full-size layout.

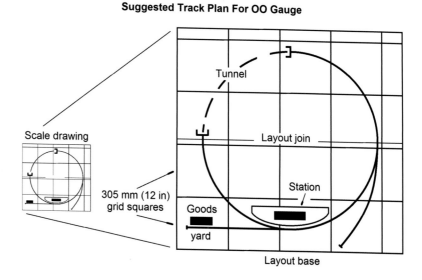

Suggested Track Plan For OO Gauge

Scale drawing

305 mm (12 in) grid squares

Tunnel

Layout join

Station

Goods yard

Layout base

Fig. 80 Transferring the track plan, drawn on tracing paper, on to the Styrofoam base using carbon paper.

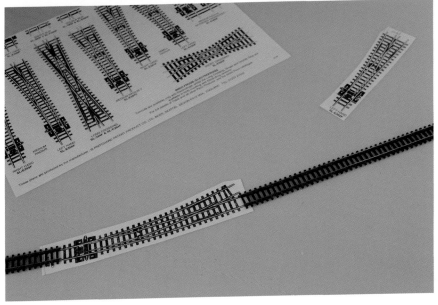

Fig. 81 Full-size Peco point templates are cut out from printed sheets and temporarily pinned down as a guide for aligning the track or, instead, the actual points can be used as a guide.

the positions of points and track, etc., onto the layout from your scale drawing using the grid lines as a guide. A useful tip here is to plot your track plan onto tracing paper, laid over the surface of the layout to enable any amendments to be made before marking on the final plot positions, using carbon paper under the tracing paper. I found this method particularly handy when using Styrofoam for the base in preventing unwanted plot lines making indentations in the surface of the foam.

To help ensure the track will eventually fit when it is laid within the space of your layout, Peco full-size paper templates of their points are available from model railway retailers in various scales and radii. The templates are cut out and temporarily pinned in place to check that curves and straight sections of track will align correctly with the points.

TEIGNSIDE QUAY

The following pages describe the building of the Teignside Quay layout, which is housed within the folding carcass.

Three semi-oval track circuits form the basis of the layout using N-scale Peco Streamline Universal Fine Code 55 flexible track, together with matching Code 55 electrofrog points. Locomotives are controlled by a four-track analogue controller produced by Gaugemaster, the fourth control on the controller unit being used to operate the working features on the layout.

Observing the suggested method in plotting the track plan described in the section Marking Out, plot the track plan, shown in Fig.83, on to the foam base of the layout. The large curves are drawn using the 'string and pin' method shown in Fig. 84.

Fig. 82   A bird's eye view of Teignside Quay with 305mm square grid lines marked on to assist positioning the track and layout features.

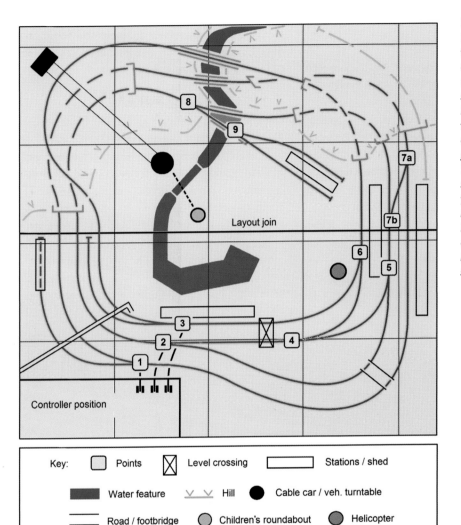

Key:
☐ Points	⊠ Level crossing	▭ Stations / shed
■ Water feature	⌄ ⌄ Hill	● Cable car / veh. turntable
— Road / footbridge	● Children's roundabout	● Helicopter

Layout join

Controller position

Fig. 83 Teignside Quay track plan is transferred full-size on to the foam base using the method shown in Fig. 80. The isolated section of track at the top-right of the layout, coloured green, is unpowered. The positions of the stations and working features, including the route of the drive shaft between the cable car and children's roundabout, are also shown.

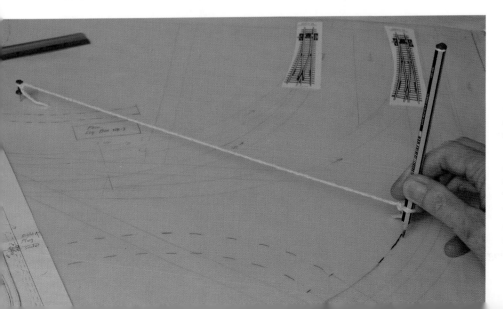

Fig. 84 The 'pin and string' method is employed for drawing the larger curves. The pin position and length of string may require adjustment to obtain a smooth transitional alignment between the curved and straight sections of track.

TRACKWORK

Before commencing track-laying, mark out the section of the river feature running under the viaduct and the two low bridges on the foam base, then carve and shape. The bottom of the river feature is almost the depth of the foam base; however, if you do inadvertently cut right through, which I did, a piece of glued-on scrap foam will make an effective repair. The remaining length of the river and basin feature can be carved out during the landscaping stage.

The three-arch viaduct, station buildings, level-crossing and platforms are constructed from commercially available plastic and card kits, produced by manufacturers such as Peco, Ratio and Metcalfe. The viaduct should be painted first before

it is permanently glued in position during the track bending and cutting stage. Station details are described in Chapter 6.

ELEVATED AND SUPER-ELEVATED TRACK

Elevated Track

The normal gradient on model railways is around 1 in 36in. However, on Teignside Quay, the gradient is rather steeper at 3in in little more than 40in. The standard height of the viaduct, which is set within the available space of the layout, is a contributory factor in this steeper gradient, although I acknowledge the gradient could possibly be made flatter by reducing the height of the viaduct by trimming the base of the viaduct pillars. In operating the layout, it

Fig. 85   This advanced overall view shows, for reference, how the completed trackwork will look in relation to the positioning of the elevated track supports and other layout features.

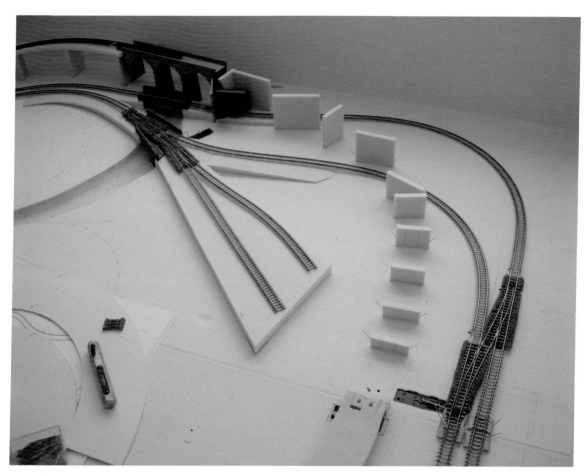

Fig. 86 The initial track-laying stage showing the positioning of the elevated foam track supports together with the raised track levels, cut and laminated from foam sheet, where the two, low, plate-girder bridges are positioned.

is interesting to watch some spinning-wheel action on one or two of my less able locomotives struggling to ascend the incline when heading up a rake of wagons. The answer here, of course, is to run a two-headed formation, whereby two locomotives are coupled together to provide more grip and pulling power. Happily, my six-axle drive Class 57 diesel loco will pull a couple of coaches confidently up and over the viaduct.

The track levels on the two low bridges spanning the river feature are raised by laminating two layers of 6mm (¼in) thick Styrofoam sheet together with pva glue and the ends sloped and feathered into the foam baseboard. For accuracy, gluing the viaduct in

position, and the associated viaduct gradient track supports, is achieved when bending and positioning the track.

Super-Elevated Track

This type of track refers to the outside rail on a bend that is set higher than the inner rail, which enables a full-size train to lean into a bend, thus maintaining a faster speed than would otherwise be possible if the track was level. For realism, the two large curves at the front of Teignside Quay are super-elevated by means of a thin, card strip, notched to follow the track radius under the outer rail of the track. The card strip is sandwiched between the underside of

Fig. 87 Trackwork on the two curves at the front of the layout are super-elevated and clearly show a train leaning into one of the curves. It should be noted that the middle of long coaches will overhang the track, thus increasing the tendency to pull coaches over if the track elevation is excessive.

Fig. 88 Strips of notched card are glued and pinned to the foam base to elevate the outer rail of the track. The pins are removed when the glue has set and the already ballasted track, shown on the left, is ready for gluing and pinning to the card elevated curve which is done at the track-laying stage.

ance can be greatly improved by painting the sides of track rails a light rust colour. This job is relatively easy to do on a small, completed layout where the track is within close reach, but can be difficult on larger layouts where one is required to lean over in a back-aching attempt to paint a distant track rail. If you do choose to paint the track before it is cut and laid, remember to scrape off all traces of paint where joining clips will be used to join track together in order to ensure electrical conductivity. Similarly, this applies to all pointwork and, importantly, the moving blade contacts on the points, which must remain shiny clean.

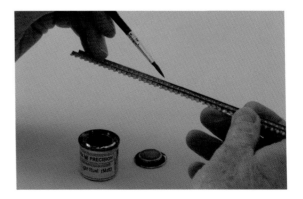

Fig. 89 Painting the track rails requires a steady hand and this task is made easier by painting the track with matt enamel paint before the track is laid. Any excess paint on the top of the rails should be wiped off with a cloth and paint scraped away where track-joining clips are to be positioned.

the track and the foam base of the layout when the final position is known when bending and cutting the track.

PAINTING THE TRACK

You may think that I am jumping the gun here and that painting the track is one of the last jobs to do on a model railway layout. In any case, you may think, 'Why paint the track at all?'; this, of course, is a matter of choice. However, the sight of shiny new metal track straight off the model shop shelf does not look very authentic, and therefore the appear-

POINTWORK

For potentially smoother running of locomotives with a short wheelbase, Peco electrofrog points are the choice for the layout. Reference numbers of these points are shown in Fig. 96. The majority of

Fig. 90 First of the three manually and remotely controlled points temporarily positioned with double-sided adhesive tape. Points 2 and 3 are positioned equally apart to correspond with the same track spacing at the level-crossing, to ensure the inner and middle sections of track are parallel. The three recessed wire-in-tube point-control linkages are glued in slots that are cut in the foam base at the track-laying stage.

Fig. 91 The completed trio of the manually controlled point levers, mounted on the switch panel, cut out from black styrene sheet and screwed next to the train controller position. Optional model flying aircraft control clevises are screwed to the point control wires, allowing adjustment of the lever positions.

the points are electrically controlled remotely from switches mounted adjacent to the train controller. However, three of the points are manually controlled because they are mounted within easy reach, close to the front of the layout.

Manually Controlled Points

Points that are numbered 1, 2 and 3 on the track plan are within easy reach and so can be remotely operated, manually employing the 'wire in tube' method, whereby track selection on the points is controlled by thin piano wire running inside an aluminium tube between the sliding tie-bar on the point and a hand-operated lever. One end of the piano wire is bent at 90 degrees to engage in the tie-bar of the point and the wire threaded through the aluminium tube, which is recessed and glued into the foam baseboard. The other end of the wire is bent to engage through a pre-drilled hole in a Peco control lever, normally used to operate signals linked with a nylon cord.

Electrically Controlled Points

The remaining points on the layout are electrically operated by solenoid action SEEP PM2 point motors, produced by Gaugemaster. These point motors are compact and have only one moving part, consisting of a horizontal sliding control bar with a solenoid at each end, which is actuated with a remotely positioned switched lever. Electrical power to the point motors is courtesy of one of the 16V AC accessory terminals located on the back of the train controller, via a capacitor discharge unit to ensure reliable operation of the points.

The point motors are suitable for mounting directly under or on top of the foam baseboard and fastened with self-tapping woodscrews with a drop of pva glue to lock the screws into the foam. Installation arrangements of the solenoid point motors are described at the track-laying stage.

CUTTING AND BENDING

In order to see how the track will look initially, before it is permanently connected and laid, the track is cut, bent and positioned loose on top of the track plan that has been drawn on to the tracing paper and laid over the foam baseboard. To start with, it is suggested that the inner and straight sections of track, from point numbers 2 and 3, to the level-crossing, are first cut to length and placed parallel to each other on the track plan. It may be helpful to assemble the level-crossing at this stage to aid track alignment through the crossing.

Cutting

To aid cutting lengths of straight sections of track using a small hacksaw, the track is supported on a wood block and held in position with a smaller wood block on top, notched to fit over the track rails. The ends of the cut rails are filed to remove any burrs to assist in being able to push on rail clips when joining the sections of track together.

Fig. 92 Cutting straight sections of track to length using a small hacksaw with the track supported on a wooden block and using a smaller block slotted to fit over the track rails to guide the saw blade. (Purpose-made rail-cutters, similar to wire-cutting pliers, are also available from model railway shops.)

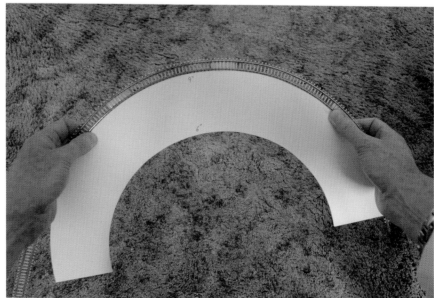

Fig. 93 Going round the bend, using the card-template method to assist even curvature of the track. Adhesive tape will help retain curvature while bending the track.

Bending

When cutting the lengths of curved sections of track, a length of flexi-track is initially bent around a template that is cut out from card. The radius of the template can either be traced onto the card from the track plan, or drawn on using a pair of compasses for small curves, or the 'pin and string' method for larger curves. The track is bent around the template and held in position with strips of adhesive tape. You will find when the track is removed from the template that it will tend to spring back a

little. This is overcome by over-bending the track, using the template as a guide.

As an aside here, when bending small-radius curves, I found it helpful to apply spots of superglue between the plastic webbing and the rails to retain track curvature.

The inner rail of the curved section of track will protrude further than the outer rail at the ends of the track, and these are cut level using the same method as described in cutting straight track, using wood blocks and a small hacksaw.

Fig. 94   Checking track curvature against the full-size track plan, marking the lengths of track that require cutting using the 'paper-point templates' as a guide.

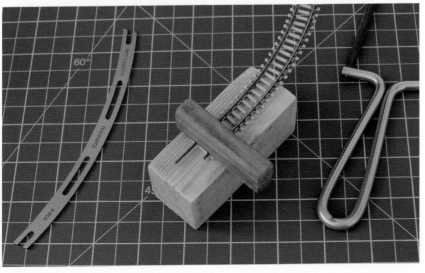

Fig. 95   Cutting the curved track. Note the protruding inner rail that occurs as the track is bent – this is cut off to match the length of the outer rail using the same cutting method in Fig. 92. Metal 'Tracksetta' templates, also shown here, produced by Melcam Models, are an alternative way to help to bend track; they are available in various radii and fit between the track rails.

TRACK-LAYING

For describing the three semi-oval track circuits, I have referred to these as follows: A, for the inner elevated-track circuit; B, for the middle-track circuit; and C, for the outer-track circuit. These letters are shown in Figs 96 and 97, and also refer to where the colour-coded track feeds that connect the electrical current from the train controller are attached to the track via dropper leads.

DROPPER LEADS AND SOLDERING

It is advisable to attach the dropper leads to the track before the track sections are joined together and the track is laid. This also applies to the layout joint connections whereby dropper leads connect the ends of the track to a multi-pin plug and socket located on each side of the layout carcass. Peco produce dropper leads that are pre-soldered to the underside of metal track-joining clips. However, to give more choice over where the dropper leads can be attached, I elected to solder my own leads directly to the outer side of the track rails. This method also enables access, if required, to the leads after the track is permanently fixed and ballasted. (See the section on Wiring the Layout, on page 73, for the type of wire to use.)

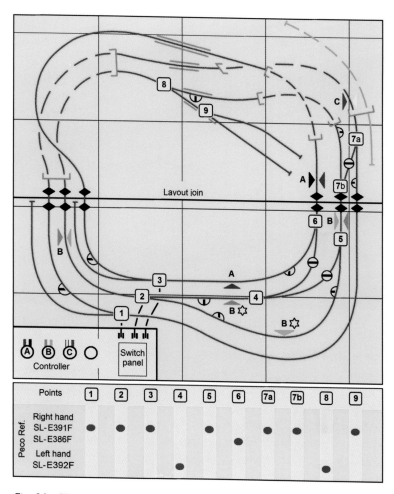

Fig. 96 *The track electrics plan shows the positions of the rail breaks and track feeds. Colour-coded dropper track feed leads, approximately 300mm (12in) in length, are attached to track sections, with dropper leads to connect the track together at the layout joint via plug and sockets. The positions of the numbered electrofrog points on the electrics plan correspond with the Peco reference numbers.*

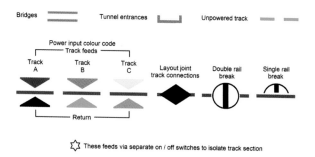

Fig. 97 *The colour-coded track and electrics key accompanies the track electrics plan, shown in Fig. 96*

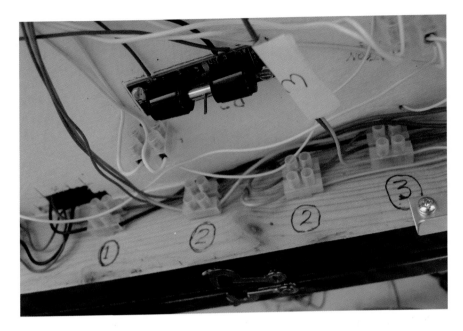

Fig. 98 Screw-type connecting blocks for connecting track wiring together are used and are fastened with screws to the inside of the layout frame. One of the flush-mounted solenoid point motors is also in view here.

It may be worth noting that the art of soldering is not a necessary requirement in constructing a model railway, and certainly where electrical wiring connections are concerned, these can be successfully joined by using screw-type connecting blocks, which are supplied in strips of around a dozen individual connectors. These can be cut to any length and mounted on most surfaces, including Styrofoam, using solvent-free contact glue. A big plus with these connectors is that, unlike soldered joints, wiring is easily altered by using a screwdriver to unscrew and redirect the appropriate wire.

If you are not familiar with the art of soldering, you may find the following basic technique adequate for most soldering jobs.

The main item required is a 25W soldering iron together with a flux-cored multicore solder, which is supplied in rolls or a handy dispenser available from hardware stores. In addition, I also use a flux paste on the wires or brass sheet to be joined to ensure that the solder flows where it is intended. A word of caution: heated flux will give off poisonous fumes, so it is advisable to work in a well-ventilated area. Make sure the wires or the surface of sheet brass to be joined is clean, using either emery or glasspaper. There are two methods of soldering. The first

method, and some would argue the better method, is to hold the solder on the joint with one hand and then, with the other hand, apply the soldering iron to melt the solder along the joint, which probably will require clamping together or finding a friend to hold the joint while it is being soldered. With the other method, melted solder is transferred onto the joint from the soldering iron. The advantage

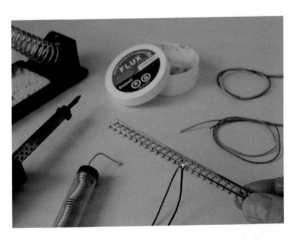

Fig. 99 Dropper wires soldered onto the outside rails of a section of track 'A'. Excess solder is filed away to just below the level of the top of the rails to prevent possible derailments.

here is that the melted solder on the soldering iron is applied with one hand, leaving the other hand free to hold the items to be joined, which makes it easier to solder wires together when scrabbling around under the layout, for example.

JOINING TRACK

To be on the cautious side, I decided to temporarily join and lay the track, together with points, and also wire the layout before the track was permanently ballasted in position, so as to remedy any possible faults in track alignment or wiring. I also decided to lay the track on pre-ballasted foam underlay, rather than use the more time-consuming traditional method of hand-ballasting with loose granite N-scale chippings. The pre-ballasted foam underlay is supplied by Gaugemaster in 5m-length rolls. The chief advantage of using this ballasted foam is that it is quick to lay and looks authentic when in place with the track. Actual scale-size granite chippings are impregnated on the shoulder surfaces of the foam and between the spaces of the track sleepers. The track sleepers themselves sit within moulded recesses in the foam.

All the track points on the layout are fitted with the ballasted foam underlay prior to positioning the points on the layout. Cut suitable lengths of the ballasted foam to cover the lengths of the points. Where the track branches out on the points, cut the foam along the middle to fit the track sleepers. The space between the branching tracks is hand-filled with granite chippings and sealed when the track is permanently fixed in position. Apply glue to the underside of the point sleepers and press the ballasted foam in place.

The best place to start laying and joining track together is by temporarily pinning the points numbered 1, 2 and 3 in position, and to construct and instal the manually operated 'wire in tube' linkages described in the section, Manually Controlled Points on page 62.

The next task is to join the track and points together, noting where the rail breaks are required, starting with the outer track circuit 'C' and leaving sufficient space for the main station platform at

Fig. 100   The pre-ballasted foam underlay supplied by Gaugemaster is cut to length from the roll and cut to fit the points.

Fig. 101   UHU glue is solvent-free and suitable for gluing the foam ballast to the underside of the point sleepers.

Fig. 102   One of the finished foam-ballasted points, which is painted before final fixing to the layout. Note the foam is cut away to allow free movement of the sliding tie-bar.

the side of the layout. The track feeds, and also the track-joining dropper wires on each side of the layout joint, are threaded through holes made with a bradawl through the foam baseboard. The two low bridges are constructed using Peco bridge sides, glued to a styrene sheet track base and temporarily pinned in position over the carved-out water feature.

Repeat the above steps for track circuit 'B', and space and hold apart the track curves by using two or three guides, which are cut from styrene sheet. The distance apart between the curves should be sufficient to allow your longest coaches to pass each other without colliding. I also used a Peco N-scale way gauge to align the space between the double tracks in front of the main station.

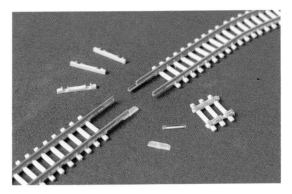

Fig. 103   To join the track sections together, cut part of the integral plastic-moulded sleeper webbing away from the rails to leave space to push on the joining clips. Scrape away any paint to ensure electrical conductivity with the metal clips. Both rails of the track sections are joined with metal joiners, except where a rail break is required to prevent a short circuit, in which case a plastic isolating clip is used as shown here.

Fig. 104   Individual Peco plastic sleepers are glued to the underside of the rails to replace the removed plastic sleeper webbing. For clarity, the plastic isolating clip for the rail break is shown here with a large gap in the rails. In practice, the gap would be about the thickness of two postcards.

Fig. 105   The layout at an advanced stage of construction. In particular it shows the positions of the viaduct and the two low bridges.

Fig. 106 *Positioning the curved track apart using guides cut from styrene sheet. The red standard Peco N-gauge way gauge is used to determine the track spacing in front of the main station.*

Fig. 107 *Tight curves. The inner track curves near the front of the layout are held in place with spots of superglue between the plastic sleeper webbing and the rails.*

Referring to Figs 85 and 86, begin laying the elevated-track circuit 'A' by first temporarily fixing in position the Peco three-arch viaduct to the foam baseboard. Connect the track sections together following the track plan, repeating the above steps for the rail breaks, track feeds and track-connecting dropper wires. At this stage the tracing paper with the track plan marked on is removed from the baseboard by sliding the paper away from the underside of the tracks.

With track circuit 'A' still in position, mark the outline of the track on the foam baseboard and then unclip and remove the track. Trace from the track plan the outline of the elevated sections of track onto a 6mm (¼in) Styrofoam sheet. This will form the base on which the elevated track is laid.

Fig. 108 *Coaches are placed on the track to double-check clearance between curves at the track-laying stage.*

Cut the foam base slightly wider than the width of the track to allow a margin for gluing the landscaping features.

Cut out the supports for the elevated track from 6mm (¼in) Styrofoam sheet and glue at equal spacing apart along the marked outline of the track on the foam baseboard. Check the continuity of the height of the supports with a straight edge and, if necessary, trim the supports to make allowances for the depth of the track base and the pre-ballasted foam underlay when it is permanently glued to the bottom of the track after the wiring is completed. The bottom end of the track base is cut and feathered into the foam baseboard at the front of the layout to make a gradual transition between levels. The track base can now be glued to the supports and to each end of the viaduct, which is now permanently glued into position. The track is now reassembled and clipped together, including the straight section on top of the viaduct.

The sidings, including the unpowered isolated section of track, are cut, bent and clipped together. Also check the clearance between the station platforms, which can be temporarily positioned at this stage, by pushing one of your longest carriages along the track.

INSTALLING THE POINT MOTORS

Dropper wires should be soldered to the contacts on the SEEP PM2 point motors, used on the layout, before they are fixed in place. There are other types of point motors equipped with spade terminals, which alleviate the necessity to solder on the wiring connections; this is an option if you wish to avoid soldering.

There are seven point motors deployed on the layout, either mounted under or on top of the foam baseboard. Where a frame member or a planned landscaping feature obstructs direct operation of the points, the point motor is fastened adjacent to the track and is fitted with a rigid connecting wire made from piano wire, the other end of which is attached to the tie-bar of the point. Detailed wiring instructions are usually included with the point motors, so excuse me for not repeating these here.

The point motors are operated via lever-type switches, mounted on a switch panel fitted adjacent to the train controller. A capacitor discharge unit is wired within the point motor circuits to increase the operating efficiency of the points. Again, wiring instructions are included with the unit.

Fig. 109 The almost completed layout showing how a coach is used to check clearance when positioning curved platforms.

Fig. 110   Cutaway view showing a point motor fastened under the foam baseboard with one of two self-tapping screws locked into the foam with pva glue applied to the screw threads. A slot is cut through the foam with a bradawl and a knife to accommodate the movement of the point motor linkage rod, the length of which is marked and the excess cut off with a hacksaw before the point motor is permanently screwed in place.

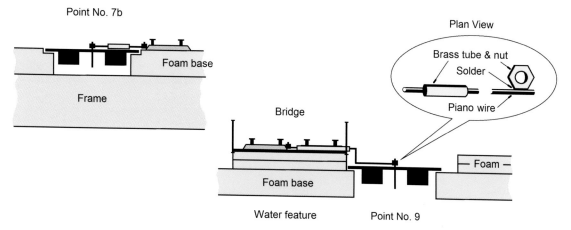

Fig. 111   Due to the position of the water feature and the baseboard frame, point numbers 7b and 9 are remotely operated by piano-wire linkages from the point motors. To hold the linkages in position, a short length of brass tubing is glued to the point motor at point No. 7b and under the track at point No. 9. Brass nuts or short lengths of brass tubing can be used and are soldered to the ends of the wire linkages. Epoxy glue can be used as an alternative to soldering, if required.

Fig. 112   Point No. 7b, shown connected to the point motor via a piano-wire linkage, will be concealed by the station platform. Point motor No. 6, indicated, is just in view and was installed prior to constructing the elevated foam track base. However, this point motor can also be fitted at the present stage by cutting away a section of the track base and gluing it back after the point motor is installed. Small wood blocks are cut to the same height as the foam ballast to which the track is pinned at the layout joint. The blocks are temporarily pinned in place at this stage and then permanently glued when the track is ballasted.

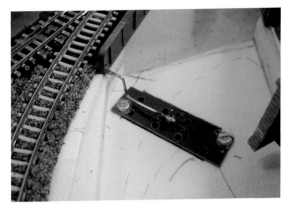

Fig. 113   The position of point No. 9 on the plate-girder bridge lies above the water feature and is operated by the stepped piano-wire linkage from the point motor, which is concealed from view at the landscaping stage.

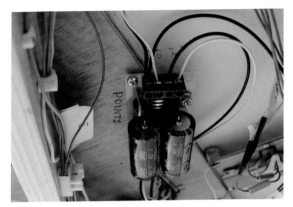

Fig. 114   A capacitor discharge unit, produced by Gaugemaster, is screwed to the underside of the train controller platform. The unit stores energy then releases it in short bursts when solenoid point motors are switched on, thus providing a firm positive movement of the points. This is particularly useful where two points at a cross-over are required to operate simultaneously, such as for point Nos 7a and 7b, for example.

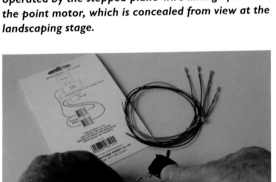

LEFT: Fig. 115   Connecting wiring to terminals on electrical items does not necessarily require soldered connections. Here a Peco wiring harness, equipped with spade-type terminals, simply pushes on to the terminals of one of the point motor operating switches.

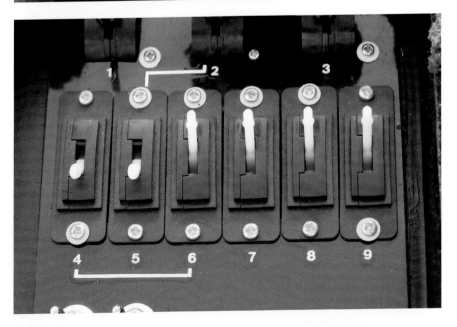

Fig. 116   Point motor lever switches mounted into the black switch panel. Point lever numbered 7 on the panel operates the two cross-over points simultaneously.

WIRING THE LAYOUT

Wiring a single-track circuit model railway layout is straightforward and the skill required could be described as on a par with connecting a light bulb to a battery – so not at all difficult. However, when it comes to wiring multi-track circuits, such as Teignside Quay, consideration has to be given to where the track feeds and rail breaks are to be located on the various sections of track. I will admit that my knowledge of model railway electrics is somewhat limited, and from what I gather, this aspect of model railway building can be bewildering for some modellers. This is an example of where joining a model railway club would be beneficial for advice and support. However, there are model railway manufacturers, such as Peco, who publish 'how to' guides, and indeed this is where I turned for information on how to wire the layout.

My initial attempt at wiring Teignside Quay turned out to be fairly successful, although I did have an issue with part of the track intermittently shorting out, which, despite my best efforts, I was unsuccessful in resolving. Looking at model railway websites for a clue to solve my problem, I discovered that the Technical Advice Bureau at Peco offers a free advice and problem-solving service to modellers, who, upon receipt of a track plan and a stamped self-addressed envelope, will provide information on where track feeds and rail breaks, etc., are required. Consequently, this resulted in me drawing a revised track electrics plan for Teignside Quay, which is shown in Figs 96 and 97.

To differentiate between the circuits on the underside of the baseboard, colour-coded wiring is used for each of the three individual track circuits, as shown in Fig. 97. In addition, wiring for the point motors and lighting can also be colour-coded. It may

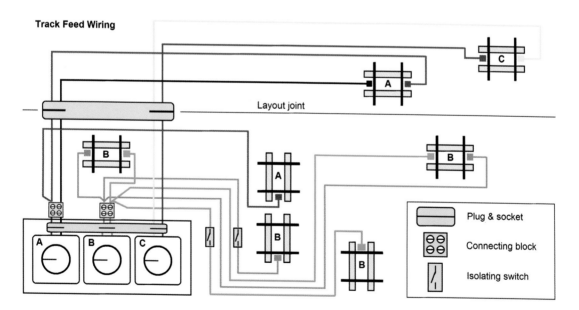

Fig. 117 *A schematic diagram showing the basic track wiring connections; it is read in conjunction with Figs 96 and 97. The track controllers are shown individually for clarity. The track dropper feed wires can be joined to the main track wiring via screw-type connecting blocks (not shown) or these can be omitted by using extra-long dropper wires. Computer type 25-way D Sub plug and sockets, available from Maplin Electronics, are used to connect the wiring across each half of the folding layout and are also used to connect the train controller to the layout. The track-isolating switches can be mounted together with the other layout switches on a panel adjacent to the train controller.*

be helpful to keep a notebook to accompany your layout for describing the colour-coded wiring circuits in case you need to make alterations to your layout in the future.

Electrical wiring for model railways is available in different colours from most model railway shops. It can be obtained by the metre or in packs of 10m-lengths. As an aside here, mains voltage wiring must not be used, as it could be confused with wiring on actual mains-operated equipment, resulting in possible danger to health.

With a portable layout, the wiring under the baseboard has to be especially secure to avoid loose or sagging wires being snagged when the layout is moved about or transported. Clips are available to secure wiring to hard surfaces, as shown in Fig. 125. In addition, I have found that Blu-Tack works well in securing wiring to the painted underside of the foam baseboard, with the advantage that wiring can easily be re-routed, if required.

TRAIN CONTROLLER

The layout is wired for 12V DC analogue control using a four-track analogue train controller. Due to the significant weight of the controller with its combined mains transformer, I decided to adapt the controller to allow it to be easily and quickly removed from the layout when it is transported

Fig. 118   The Maplin D Sub plug with the cover removed, showing the short lengths of colour-coded wires soldered to the plug and connected to the terminal strip on the back of the train controller; silicone tubing is used to keep the wires tidy.

Fig. 119   The socket for the controller plug is screwed to the platform in a position to align with the controller plug.

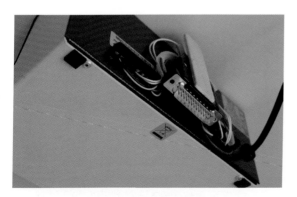

Fig. 120   A finger-grip is cut from plywood and glued to the cover of the controller plug to assist its removal when the controller is positioned on the layout.

Fig. 121   The controller plug is accessed from the top of the layout by pulling the plug out using the plywood finger grip.

and more efficient method is to wire a multi-pin plug and socket between the controller terminals and the layout wiring. The plug is wired directly to the controller terminals with short, colour-coded wires soldered to the plug, while the corresponding socket is screwed to the base of the controller platform on the layout. The socket is positioned so the plug on the controller engages with the socket when placing the controller on the platform.

LAYOUT JOINT WIRING

To enable both halves of the track circuits to receive electrical power, dropper leads from the ends of the tracks are connected via screw-type terminal blocks to a multi-pin plug and socket, mounted on each side of the layout. The sockets are screwed directly to the sides of the layout adjacent to the layout joint and the plugs are pushed by hand into the sockets. Aluminium tube is glued to widened-out cable anchorage points on the inside of each half of the plastic plug-and-socket covers to provide a collar onto which reinforced ribbed plastic tube is glued. The reinforced tubing is the type used on pond pumps, and protects the track and point motor wiring between the plug and sockets through corresponding aluminium tubing, glued through pre-drilled holes in the sides of the layout. The plug and socket wiring is terminated at screw-type connecting blocks, which are screwed on the inside of the layout frame.

Fig. 122   You are in control. General view of the control centre on the completed layout. Access to the controller connecting plug, which is secured to the back of the controller with a plastic cable tie, is via a removable panel, covered with scatter grass to match the surrounding landscape. The controller mains cable and plug is routed through the large hole. Take care not to damage the cable; connecting an RCD adapter to the mains supply is advisable. The miniature track-plan, mounted behind clear Perspex, displays the numbered points that correspond with numbered point levers.

or stored away. The back of the controller is generously equipped with an array of screw-type connecting terminals into which the wiring for the tracks, point motors and the working features are connected. Understandably then, having to unscrew each terminal to release the wiring every time the controller is removed would be inconvenient, and possibly wiring could be reconnected to the wrong terminals by mistake. A somewhat tidier

Fig. 123   The layout connecting plug and socket arrangement. A 25-way D Sub socket is screwed directly to each side of the layout. The ribbed, pond, pump-type reinforced plastic tube, which protects the wiring, is available from aquatic retailers.

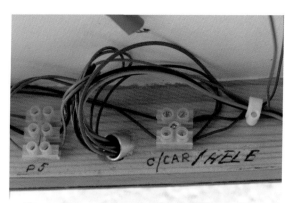

Fig. 124   One side is shown of the layout joint connecting wires soldered to the pins on one of the plugs. Unlike the sockets, the plugs are not screwed to layout sides. Short lengths of aluminium tubing are glued to the nearside plastic plug covers on to which the ribbed plastic tubing is glued. This arrangement is repeated for the socket side of the layout. Besides the track wiring, the plug and socket also connects the wiring for the point motors on the back half of the layout.

Fig. 125   The underside view of the layout showing the plug side of the wiring, terminating at screw-type connecting blocks. Note the aluminium tube, glued through the side of the layout to accept the other end of ribbed plastic tube to protect the wiring. This arrangement is repeated for the socket side of the layout.

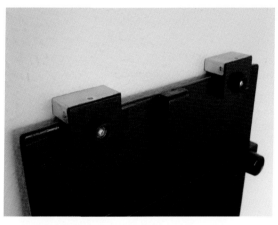

With the layout folded, the exposed disconnected plugs and sockets are vulnerable to damage and, therefore, holster-style covers are cut out and bent from aluminium sheet and screwed to wood blocks mounted to both ends of the layout protection panel. This enables the plugs to be stowed away, as shown in Figs 52 and 71.

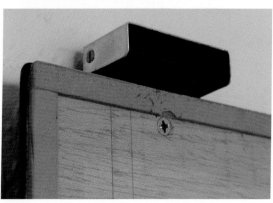

ABOVE LEFT: *Fig. 126   Aluminium sheet, holster-style covers to protect the plug and sockets on the sides of the layout are cut to suit the size of the plug and sockets, and are mounted on wooden blocks on both ends of the layout protection panel.*

LEFT: *Fig. 127   Shown is one of the four wooden block-mounted plug and socket protection covers, which are fastened with screws from the underside of the layout protection panel.*

*Fig. 128 A simple
method for connecting
the electrical supply for
the lighting from the
train controller, across
to the back half of the
layout. This arrangement
would also be suitable
for the point motor feed
circuit.*

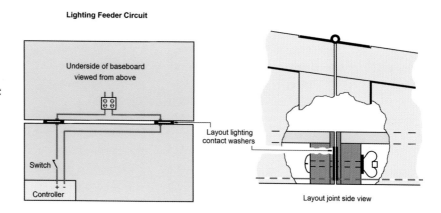

Lighting Wiring

Referring to Figs 58 and 59, the steel washers located at the layout joint-fastening holes support the electrical wiring connections between the two halves of the layout. The wiring is attached to the steel washers by stripping off the insulation and twisting the bare end of the wire around one of the washer mounting screws, thus sandwiching the wire between the washer and the layout frame. Electrical contact is made when the opened-out layout is fastened in position.

Alternative Layout Joint Wiring Connections

This option uses a plug-and-socket screw terminal arrangement, thus avoiding the need to solder wires onto multi-pin plugs and sockets. The terminal strips are comprised of twelve individual screw terminals that plug together. They can be cut to any length depending on the wiring requirements, and they could be screwed directly to the side of the layout on each side of the joint, or underneath the layout on each half of the framework at the layout joint.

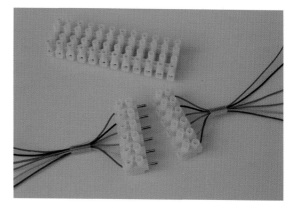

Fig. 129 This versatile plug-and-socket screw-type terminal strip is a viable alternative to using the multi-pin soldered plug and socket. The Camdenboss 6A plug and socket should be available through model railway retailers or online from Rapid Electronics Ltd.

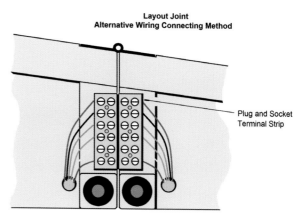

Fig. 130 Diagram to show the suggested position for the plug and socket terminals. A longer terminal strip with additional contacts could also accommodate wiring for the lighting and point motor circuits.

THE DRY RUN

All systems go… well, hopefully! This is the stage where I could try one or two of my eagerly acquired locomotives to test the integrity of the track circuits, both physically and electrically, before the track is permanently fixed and ballasted in place. Any problems with badly aligned track joints or having to reposition track feeds, for example, should be done now, otherwise some heavy-duty excavating may be required after the track has been permanently fixed and the landscaping has dried rock-hard. This could be particularly inconvenient where track may need raising and cutting to insert or to relocate plastic insulating rail-joining clips.

PERMANENT TRACK BALLASTING

When I first started building Teignside Quay, I made a point to record and photograph the various parts of the layout during each stage of its construction. However, in my haste to progress the build, I omitted to photograph in detail the initial construction of the back-left corner of the layout; in particular, the elevated track base and its supports, which are fabricated on the original layout using Styrofoam. This omission, however, did present me with the opportunity to recreate a mock-up of this corner of the layout using foam board for constructing the elevated track base and its supports, which enabled me to compare the use of these two types of foam material.

The foam board I used on the mock-up is available from hobby stores and online in various sheet sizes of 3mm, 5mm and 10mm thickness. The board consists of a paper-surfaced, rigid foam core and will accept pva and non-solvent contact glue. It is equally as lightweight as Styrofoam and due to the additional bonded paper surface, which incidentally is suitable for painting without prior preparation, is slightly stronger; however, it cannot be easily carved.

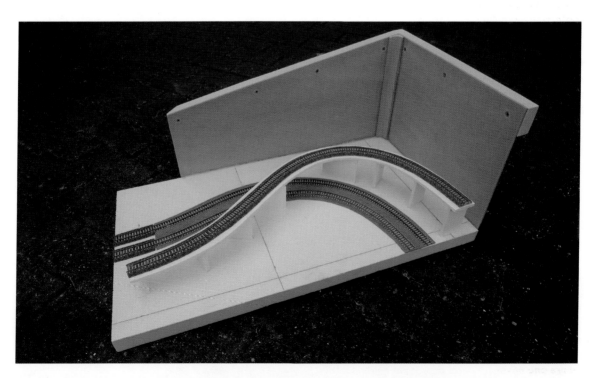

Fig. 131   Paper-faced foam board of 5mm (³⁄₁₆in) thickness can be used for constructing the elevated track base and supports as an alternative to using Styrofoam, as shown on this mock-up corner section of the layout.

Fig. 132   A curved strip of cork for the track base is cut out from 1.5mm (¹/₁₆in) thickness cork sheet and is glued with pva adhesive to the foam baseboard of the layout where the hill tunnels will be located. Card can also be used as an alternative to cork.

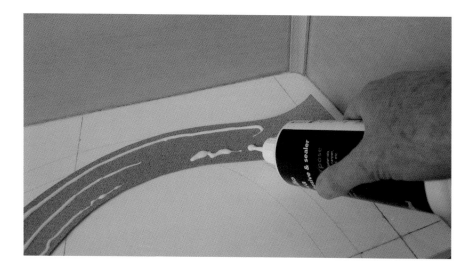

Fig. 133   The twin curved tracks that run under the tunnels are contact-glued to the cork track base and the distance between the two tracks checked with a way gauge or with coaches placed on the track to check clearance.

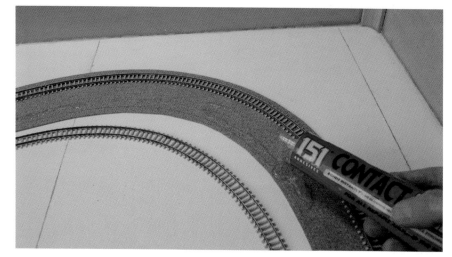

Fig. 134   Track level is maintained between the pre-ballasted foam underlay and the cork track base. Pencil marks denote where one of the tunnel entrances will be located.

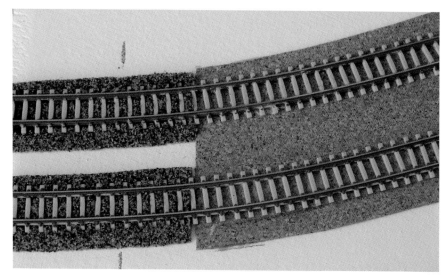

CORK TRACK BASE

Because part of the track is hidden from view under the hills, it is unnecessary and uneconomical to lay pre-ballasted foam underlay for these sections of track. The purpose of the cork, apart from reducing the sound of the trains running on the track, is to provide a raised base on which the track is laid to match the adjoining level of the pre-ballasted foam track underlay.

PRE-BALLASTED FOAM UNDERLAY

This is supplied in 5m rolls; to make it more manageable, it is suggested this is cut into approximately 300mm (12in) lengths. Each length is inserted under the track and pressed in between the track sleepers. Some of the track sections may require unclipping first and carefully pulling apart to enable the ballasted foam underlay to be inserted under

the track. Pins are used to hold the foam-ballasted track in position on curves. Diluted pva glue of about half water and half pva, with a couple of drops of washing-up liquid to help the solution to soak in, is liberally applied to the foam-ballasted track with a squeezy-type dispenser. Apply sufficient diluted glue to penetrate through the ballasted foam on to the track base using a brush. The track-joining clips should be kept dry, if possible, by covering them with tape while the track is being glued. Clean the track rails with a damp cloth before the glue is fully set, which will be about 24 hours. This same method of fixing the track and the pre-ballasted foam underlay to the layout base also applies to the points. Gaps in the foam-ballasted points are filled in with granite ballast chippings and fixed with diluted pva glue, taking care not to glue the moving parts.

Fig. 135 Feeding a length of pre-ballasted foam underlay, available from Gaugemaster, under the track.

Fig. 136 Pins hold the track in position, while diluted pva glue is applied with a squeeze bottle to the pre-ballasted foam underlay.

Fig. 137 A brush is used to spread and stipple in the diluted pva glue to ensure the glue penetrates right through to the track base. The rails are wiped clean with a damp cloth before the glue sets.

Fig. 138 N-gauge granite chippings, to match the pre-ballasted foam underlay, are applied with a teaspoon into the gaps between the point sleepers, brushed in place and sealed with diluted pva glue.

CHAPTER SIX

BUILDINGS AND LANDSCAPING

This is where one's imagination and artistic ambitions can be fulfilled. Of course this does not necessarily apply to layouts that faithfully reproduce an actual present or past prototypical railway, although the majority of layouts share similar landscaping construction techniques. Apart from the track arrangement, water and cable-car features on my wish-list for Teignside Quay, I had little idea what other features to include on the layout. My initial thought was to populate the remaining spaces with trees and grassed areas, which certainly would be relatively quick and easy to accomplish, but not very inspiring. It was not until after I had installed the stations and marked out the water feature, completed the hill structures and the cable-car feature, that ideas formed on how roads could be developed and, in turn, where buildings and additional working features would eventually be included. It may be said

the term 'landscaping' applies to predominantly green areas of a layout, comprising hills, trees and fields. However, as the working cable-car arrangement forms an integral part of the landscape, I have included the construction details of this working feature in this chapter.

The various landscaping stages are described under the following headings: stations, tunnels and hills, cable car, buildings and locations, roads and bridges, water features and green areas.

STATIONS

By now you may have acquired and painted your choice of stations and platforms, and have temporarily positioned them on the layout. It may be worth noting that, although these items do not individually weigh very much, it is surprising how

Fig. 139 Station platforms are fastened in position with small countersunk woodscrews into wood blocks, glued to the foam baseboard. The lighting connecting wires for the platform and station buildings are a push fit into aluminium or brass tubes inserted through the baseboard.

the weight can mount up, especially if using several 'off-the-shelf' readymade resin-moulded buildings. Plastic and card kits of buildings, on the other hand, are comparatively lightweight and ideally suited for a portable layout. Generally, station platforms and buildings are glued permanently on the layout. However, one of the features I had included on my wish-list was to instal lighting on the platforms and in some of the buildings. Therefore, it was desirable to devise a method by which the platforms and

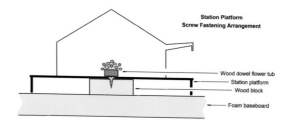

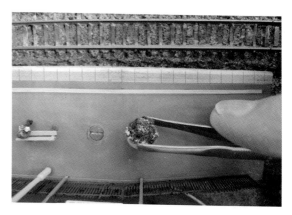

TOP: **Fig. 140** Diagram showing cross-section view of the platform fastening arrangement.

MIDDLE: **Fig. 141** Flower power! Flowers are represented with dabs of painted landscaping foliage, glued to tubs made from wood dowel. Waiting passenger seems blissfully unaware of approaching giant finger.

Fig. 142 The small shelter covers the other platform fastening screw. The footbridge is secured to the platforms with small screws through the back edge of the footbridge base only so they cannot be seen when the layout is viewed from the front.

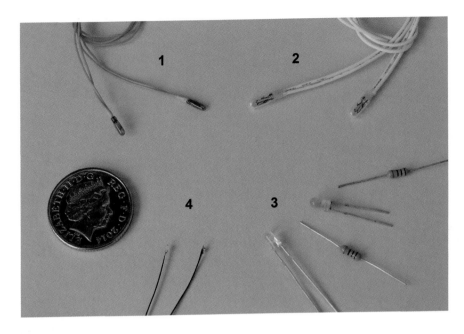

Fig. 143 Examples of 12V bulbs used on the layout, shown against a ten-pence piece for size comparison: (1) 2mm 'grain of rice' bulb; (2) 3mm 'grain of wheat' bulb; (3) 3mm LEDs with 100K ohm resistors; (4) 1mm 'nano' size LEDs also require resistors.

station buildings could easily be removed from the layout to gain access to wiring and light bulbs or LEDs. After some head scratching, I decided that the quickest and most secure way was simply to screw the platforms to the layout using small countersunk woodscrews. Wood blocks cut to the internal height of the platforms were glued to the baseboard and the platforms screwed to the wood blocks. Flower tubs, to disguise the screw heads, were made from wood dowel and planted with glued-on painted landscaping foliage to represent flowers. Blu-Tack was used to secure the tubs on to the screw heads simply.

STATION LIGHTING

There are two main types of lighting for model railways: miniature 12V filament bulbs and LEDs. Filament bulbs produce a less harsh-looking light than LEDs and are akin to household filament bulbs in the real world. Whilst LEDs, which emit a white light, on the other hand, are similar to fluorescent lighting. The light intensity of bulbs can be varied according to the output voltage of the power source or how they are wired, which is useful for emulating gas lighting, for example. LEDs last longer than bulbs but most LEDs require a resistor to be soldered into

the supply circuit to reduce the operating current, otherwise they will burn out if connected directly to the power source.

Commercially produced working lamp-columns are available to reflect different periods in time, from ornate Victorian to modern minimalist designs. I decided to have a go at constructing my

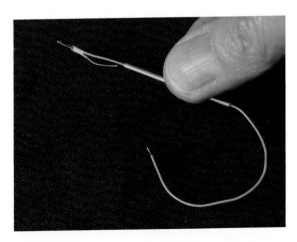

Fig. 144 Constructing a lamp-column using 1mm-diameter aluminium tube and a coloured 'grain of rice' bulb. One of the two bulb wires is cut short and the insulation removed to provide the electrical contact when bulb wire is pushed inside the tube.

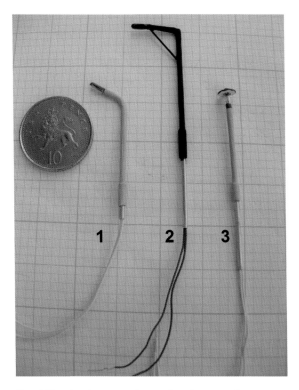

Fig. 145 A selection of completed station lamp-columns made from 1mm-diameter aluminium tube: (1) simple modern design; (2) older bracket style; (3) modern-style lamp-column using thin styrene sheet for the top, cut out with a hole punch.

own working lamp-columns, mainly for financial reasons, as I reckon they could be made at fraction of the cost of 'off-the-shelf' offerings. Basically, all that is required is an aluminium tube of about 1mm diameter, cut to form the height, including the mounting depth, of a lamp-column. The modern style of lamp-column is the easiest to make, being either straight with a bulb perched on top, or the type of column with a curved arm. 12V 'grain of rice' size of bulbs are wired into the tops of the aluminium tubing, with one of the insulated wires threaded right though inside the tube; the remaining bulb wire is cut short and the insulation removed to make electrical contact inside the aluminium tube, which serves as an electrical conductor when the wire is pushed inside the tube. Similarly, contact at the base of the tube is made by pushing thin connecting wire, with the insulation stripped off, into the tube. The bulbs are secured in the tubes with a spot of superglue and filler is applied to any gaps at the base of the bulbs; the columns are then painted, after smoothing off the filler. Sooner or later the odd bulb or two is bound to blow, and as the bulbs are an integral part of the lamp-column, it seemed sensible to make a few spares.

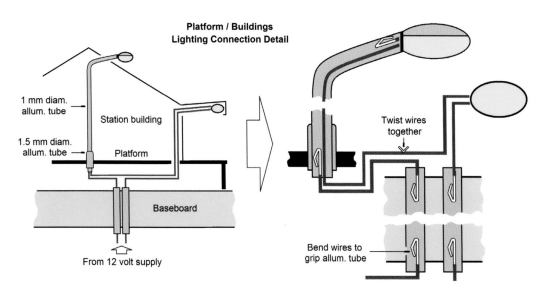

Fig. 146 Suggested method for constructing the lamp-columns without having to solder the 12V bulbs and column wiring connections.

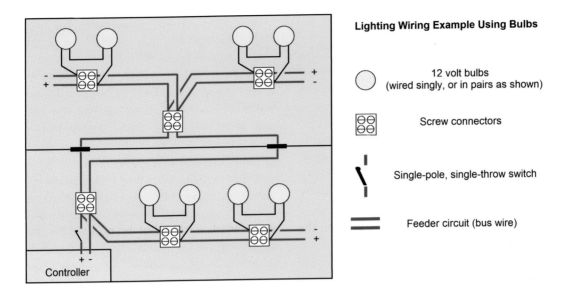

Lighting Wiring Example Using Bulbs

12 volt bulbs
(wired singly, or in pairs as shown)

Screw connectors

Single-pole, single-throw switch

Feeder circuit (bus wire)

Controller

ABOVE: *Fig. 147 The majority of the 12V bulbs on the layout are wired in pairs (in series) to reduce the level of light output to a more realistic glow. However, if one of the pair of bulbs blows, the circuit is broken and therefore the remaining bulb will go out. Alternatively, clear or coloured LEDs can be used – they also last longer than bulbs.*

BELOW: *Fig. 148 The working Victorian-style platform lamp-columns are fashioned from aluminium tube, household fusewire, styrene sheet and filler. The station building is a readymade resin-moulded product with the canopy constructed from a plastic kit and housing a bulb to illuminate the front of the building.*

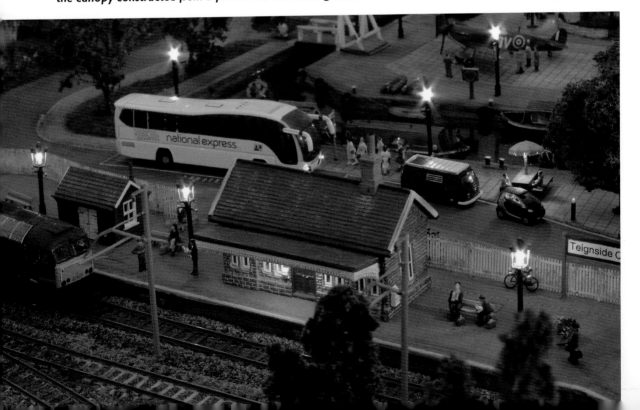

To reduce the voltage and therefore make the bulbs emit a less harsh light, the platform and station lighting bulbs were connected in pairs to a feeder (bus wire). As to the maximum number of bulbs that can be wired on the layout, this is one of those 'how long is a piece of string' questions, and is one of those occasions where I deployed my trusted 'trial and error' approach by temporarily connecting the bulbs to see what the effect would be. If one of the bulbs dimmed on a circuit, then I would either back-track or experiment in trying something else. Problems can arise, however, if bulbs of different voltage or size are used on the same circuit; consequently resistors will probably need to be wired into the circuit. An assortment of various resistors come in handy for these occasions and I would also suggest an appropriately rated fuse is wired between the power source and the lighting circuit.

Alternatively, if you don't want the bother of taking the DIY lighting route, then there is the option of using commercially produced 12V lighting kits, such as the type used in dolls' houses. Hornby produce lighting kits for OO-scale model railways, comprising of a fused wiring harness, bulbs and extension sockets, which I suggest could also be used to illuminate N-scale buildings internally.

Internally illuminated buildings should be a snug fit on the ground to prevent unwanted light from showing though any gaps. Some 'off-the-shelf' readymade resin buildings, when lit from inside, can produce a ghostly appearance with glowing walls, which is remedied by painting the insides of the walls and roof with black paint. Access to bulbs in buildings can be via a removable roof or by fixing the buildings to the ground with hidden screws, although I found it easier to glue resin buildings directly to the ground and cut a hole under the baseboard to gain access into the buildings to replace a bulb.

Fig. 149   The underside of the styrene top to the platform lamp is painted white to reflect light downwards.

Fig. 150   Access to inside the signal box, constructed from a Ratio and Wills plastic kit, is through the removable roof, held on with Blu-Tack. Bulb wiring is concealed out of sight from the windows by running the wiring along inside of one inside corners of the building.

TUNNELS AND HILLS

TUNNELS

For the layout I used Peco plastic single- and double-track tunnel mouths and retaining walls. Before gluing these permanently in position, I lined the inside of the tunnel mouths with thin styrene sheet to hide the inside construction of the hills. I also highlighted some of the moulded stonework on the tunnel faces with dabs of stone-coloured paint. Strips of rigid foam were glued around the inside edges of the tunnel mouths to enable the gluing of the ends of copper-wire armatures into the hill shell construction. Some of the tunnel mouths and the retaining walls can be glued directly to the foam baseboard, while others, particularly on the elevated section of track, are supported and glued

on pieces of rigid foam, which are glued to each side of the elevated track base.

HILLS

Hill structures are traditionally constructed from plaster cloth over a supporting card and paper membrane, expanded polystyrene carved blocks, chicken wire or screwed-up paper. Where track-work runs through tunnels, then obviously hollow hills are necessary and, therefore, a thin lightweight shell is required that is strong enough to support trees, buildings and working street lighting.

Whilst researching information on building model railway layouts before I commenced Teignside Quay, I came across a method whereby hill shells can be constructed using a similar technique to papier mâché. I remember from my schooldays making a

Fig. 151   Thin styrene sheet to hide the inside of the hill construction is glued to the backs of the tunnel mouths using plastic solvent. The inside of the styrene sheet is either painted dark grey or Metcalfe printed brick-effect paper can be glued on.

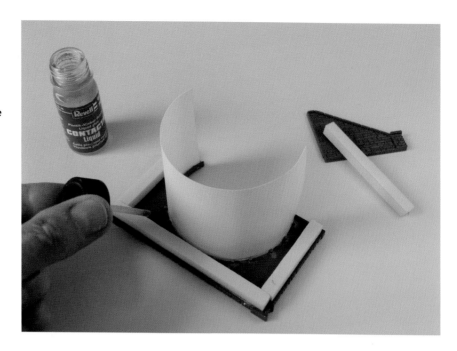

Fig. 152   The ends of the copper-wire armatures to support the laminated shell are glued into strips of rigid foam, which are glued around the back edges of the tunnel mouths.

Fig. 153 The almost completed hill sub-structure. Cotton thread is tied to hold the copper-wire armatures together. Now the outline structure of the hill is known, a pad saw is used to cut out the opening in the back of the layout carcass for accessing the tracks, via a hinged plywood cover, which is screwed on the outside. A similar access is cut out in the side of the layout carcass under the cable-car hill and a hinged plywood cover fitted.

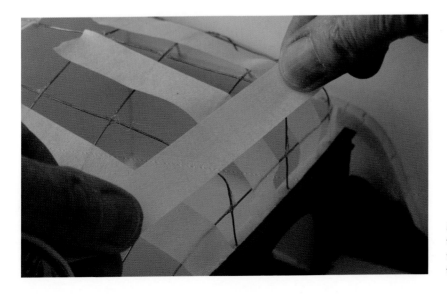

Fig. 154 Strips of masking tape are applied over the wire armatures to support the laminated shell.

Fig. 155   A half water and half pva glue solution is used to soak, with a brush, four layers of kitchen towel together. (See Rice (2007), where the author describes this method.)

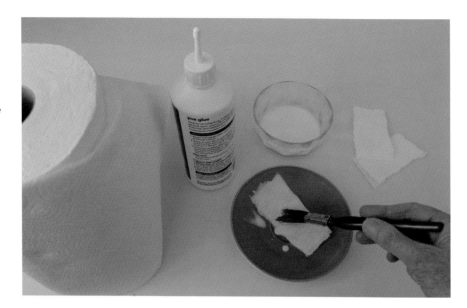

mask by mixing paste and torn-up pieces of newspaper together and finding how light and strong the mask was when it had dried. I decided to try a similar method for making the hill shell at the back of the layout, using more absorbent kitchen towel rather than newspaper.

The hill sub-structure at the back right-hand corner of the layout is constructed from 6mm (¼in) rigid foam, the height of which is first marked on the inside of the back corner and a strip of rigid foam bent and glued to the marked line. The flat top of the hill and its supports are made from rigid foam and glued to the baseboard, allowing sufficient clearance for your longest coaches on the curves. Pieces of sheet foam are glued to the baseboard to raise and pack up the ground level, where required, prior to constructing the hill shell.

I used copper wire (stripped from household mains earth cable) for forming the hill contours and is what I would call the 'bird cage method', whereby

Fig. 156   Lay the glue-soaked solution of kitchen towel pieces all over the sub-structure, overlapping and moulding them using a brush.

Fig. 157 The partially completed hill. Note the polythene bags stuffed into the tunnel mouths to protect the track from dripping glue. Compare hill structure with Figs 26 and 105.

lengths of copper wire are bent and glued vertically and horizontally to form an armature, the ends of which are glued into the rigid foam hill top, including tunnel mouth sides and the foam strip around the back inside corner of the layout. Strips of masking tape are applied to partially fill the copper-wire grid prior to laminating on the kitchen towel shell.

To form the hill shell, four layers of kitchen towel are stacked together and torn into about 25mm (1in) wide strips and soaked in a dish containing a solution of half water and half pva glue. The glue-soaked strips are then placed and moulded with a brush over the copper armature. This procedure is repeated with more overlapping glue-soaked strips until the 'bird cage' is completely covered.

The top of the hill at the back left-hand corner of the layout is constructed from thick rigid foam so

Fig. 158 Inside the hill sub-structure viewed from the hinged door, which is secured with a magnetic catch (see also Fig. 70). The glued hill shell is strong enough to allow some of the foam elevated track supports to be cut away to improve access to the tracks. The unpowered track (fiddle yard) in the foreground is used to store and change trains.

it can be carved to shape and is glued to the inside corner of the layout. The inside edge of the foam is cut to follow the curvature of the elevated track section below. For the face of the hillside cutting, tree bark provides a lightweight authentic exposed-rock appearance. The bark is available in various shapes and sizes and is cut to the approximate thickness of sliced bread, and is glued in between recesses, cut into the foam hill top and the elevated track base below. The clearance between carriages or locomotives and the edges of the rock face should be checked at this stage. Filler is applied and sculpted to blend the rock face with the hill top, which is carved to shape. Card is cut and glued between the hill top and elevated track base to form the remaining face of the hill cutting.

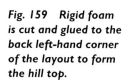

Fig. 159 Rigid foam is cut and glued to the back left-hand corner of the layout to form the hill top.

Fig. 160 Cork bark, produced by Jordan, is used to represent the rock face and is continued to the three-arch viaduct.

Fig. 161   Gaps between the cork bark and hill top are filled in with cellulose or acrylic filler, which is sculpted when almost dry to blend with the bark. The remaining hill cutting face is covered with card to provide a base for gluing on Metcalfe printed paper brickwork to represent a retaining wall.

Fig. 162   This busy view of part of the completed layout shows how the cable car sits within the landscape. There is an unintentional arch theme going on here, with the viaduct and tunnel arches being replicated on the cable-car base station, enabling moving cars to be seen on the underground section of the rotating roadway. The children's roundabout at the right of the picture is driven from the cable-car base station motor through bevel gears on a shaft linkage.

CABLE CAR

I particularly wanted to include a working cable-car feature on the layout as an alternative to watching the trains going by. In addition, I also had in mind a 'rolling road' feature, as shown in Fig.10. However, I eventually abandoned this idea, as this method of creating a moving vehicle illusion by means of a conveyor belt system seemed overly complicated for the effect I wanted to achieve. I therefore devised a relatively simple alternative, whereby a reasonably convincing effect could be achieved by fixing scale vehicles to a rotating turntable, powered by the same motor that operates the cable-car mechanism and, unlike the conveyor belt idea, it would be a relatively straightforward task to instal fibre-optic cables for the working headlights on the vehicles. The cable-car motor could also power a children's roundabout via bevel gears on a shaft linkage, although the idea

for this feature, and also for a helicopter with rotating blades, did not materialize until the layout was almost completed.

CABLE-CAR MECHANISM

Two cable cars are attached with hooks to a continuous nylon thread loop, suspended between two pulley wheels, one of which is powered by an electric-geared motor housed under the base station. It is not critical where exactly the cable-car arrangement is located on the layout; however, the position for the vehicle turntable opening, which is cut out of the foam baseboard, should not be obstructed by any of the timber-frame members. Foam sheet is glued to the baseboard to raise the mounting height of the plywood-base station platform to provide sufficient space under the baseboard for the geared motor. The semi-circular plywood platform for the base station is cut to a larger diameter

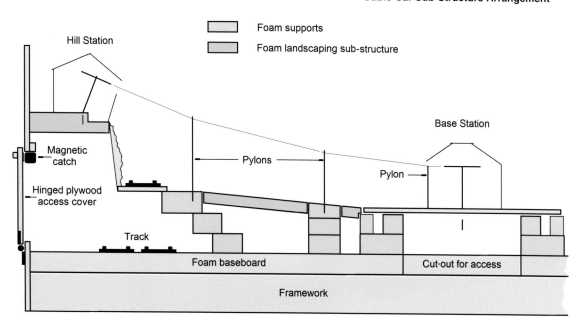

Cable-Car Sub-Structure Arrangement

Fig. 163 The arrangement of rigid foam blocks, cut from foam sheet, provides the pylon and base station supports. Gaps between the supports are filled in with foam sheet upon which the landscaping is formed. Access to track under the hill is by a hinged plywood cover over an opening that is cut in the side of the layout carcass.

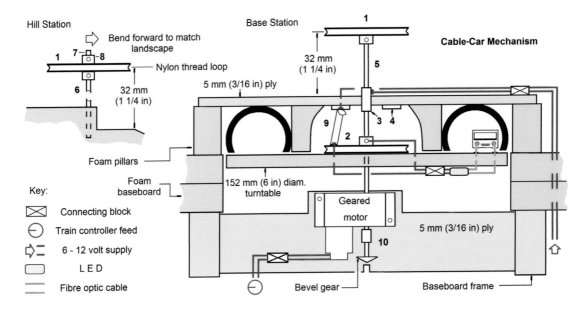

Fig. 164 *Construction detail of the base station. The geared motor, pulleys and bevel gears can be obtained online from W. Hobby Ltd and also from Technobots. Rigid foam is mostly used for the construction, apart from the base and motor mount, which are made from plywood for strength. The legend to the diagram numbers are as follows: (1) 25mm (1in) diameter plastic pulley; (2) 25mm (1in) diameter plastic pulley for turntable/spring contact mounting; (3) 10g. inside diameter (i/d) brass tube bearing; (4) steel washer contact; (5) 10g. outside diameter (o/d) brass tube shaft; (6) 10g. i/d brass tube support; (7) 10g. o/d brass tube spindle; (8) pulley retaining collar; (9) brass sheet contact; (10) 10g. i/d brass tube coupling for children's roundabout drive shaft.*

Fig. 165 *The completed base station with cars on the rotating turntable roadway, powered by the cable-car motor.*

RIGHT: **Fig. 166   The foam base station sub-structure is constructed around the turntable opening, cut into the baseboard. Strips of card are cut and glued to the foam hub and sub-base to hide the gap on the edge of the turntable when it is finally installed.**

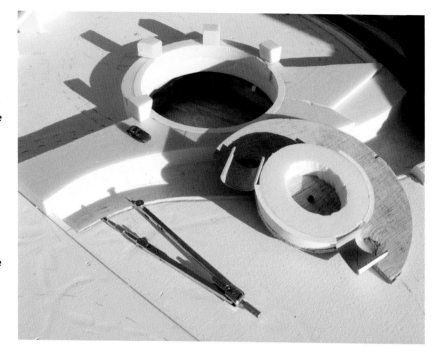

BELOW: **Fig. 167 Temporarily screw the base station platform to the foam supporting pillars to check the alignment of the vehicle turntable with a length of brass tubing.**

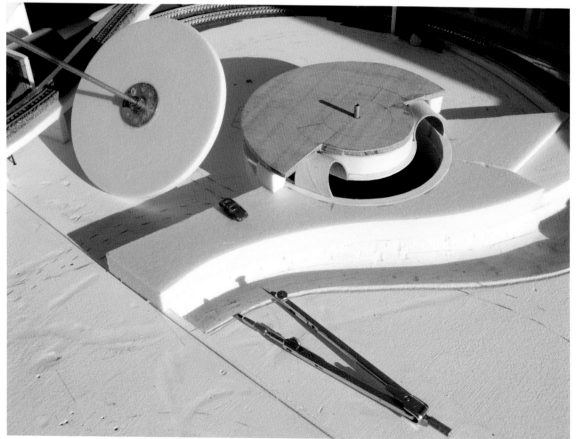

Fig. 168 *A steel washer is screwed to the underside of the platform for the vehicle fibre-optics electrical contact arm. The inside of the card tube tunnel mouths are lined with stone-effect printed paper.*

Fig. 169 *Top view of the platform with one of the fibre-optic LED feed wires connected to the steel washer with a nut and bolt, while the remaining wire is soldered to the brass tube turntable shaft bearing. The rock face is formed by sculpting filler with a knife, while the tunnel faces are painted brick-embossed plastic sheet.*

than the vehicle turntable to enable it to be glued to foam supporting pillars. Tunnel entrances are cut out from suitably sized card tubes and glued to an inner foam core, which is glued to the plywood platform. The centre of the foam core is hollowed out to accommodate the steel electrical contact washer/spring arrangement and the motor shaft turntable fastening.

Rigid foam is suitable for constructing the vehicle turntable, being lightweight and easy to work with in respect of fitting the vehicles and the associated fibre optics. The centre of the turntable is reinforced with a glued-on plastic pulley wheel with a screw fastening to allow the turntable to be adjusted on the motor/gearbox shaft. Also, the pulley wheel provides a firm base on which to bolt the spring electrical wiper-arm, which is cut from brass sheet. The motor mount is constructed from plywood and is secured between the baseboard frame members with screws to allow adjustment to the alignment of the turntable by tightening or slackening the screws. The motor is wired to the spare locomotive control on the train controller via the plug and socket at the layout joint, thus providing fine adjustment in controlling the speed and even reversing the direction of the cable cars. Wiring

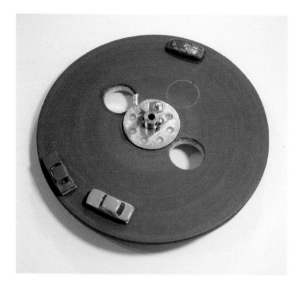

Fig. 170 On my prototype cable car, I used a metal shaft fastening plate and inserted plastic insulating washers between the bolted-on brass spring wiper-arm and the metal plate to prevent a short circuit. A plastic screw-on type pulley wheel will negate the requirement for fitting insulation washers.

Fig. 171 Thin fibre-optic cables are routed through the plastic vehicle chassis from the underside of the pre-painted turntable and the ends of the cables are glued into drilled-out holes in the headlights of the vehicle bodies. The LED and fibre-optic cables for the vehicles are glued and taped to the underside of the turntable.

Fig. 172 Prior to bolting the motor to its plywood mounting, I packed the gearbox with grease to reduce the noise of the gears.

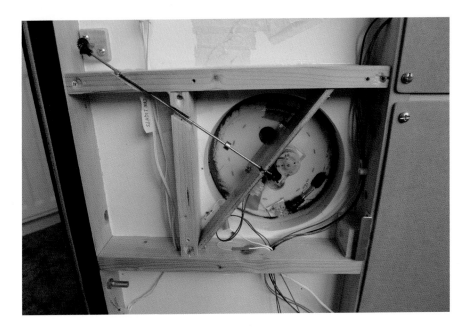

Fig. 173 Access to the motor and turntable is from underneath the layout. A couple of additional timber battens are screwed between the existing frame members to support the plywood motor mounting. The bevel geared shaft from the motor drives a children's roundabout, which was installed later as an afterthought.

to the fibre-optic cable headlights on the vehicles is taken from the lighting circuit of the layout, via the moving spring contact wiper-arm and LED. To gain access to the spring contact arrangement, the pulley wheel on the top of the drive motor gear shaft is removed and the plywood motor mount unscrewed to allow the turntable to be withdrawn from underneath the layout. The hill station pulley arrangement is freewheeling and is angled to align with the nylon thread loop. The three pylons guide the nylon thread loop in a shallow curve, with the third pylon at the base station entrance also guiding the nylon thread on to the motorized pulley wheel.

Fig. 174 The two pylon arms are bent from piano wire to guide the nylon thread on to the drive motor pulley. An LED spotlight, mounted on the pylon, and a coloured bulb are wired within the base station mechanism for night-time operation.

Fig. 175   One of the two cable cars entering the base station. The Z-shaped hook that attaches the cars to the nylon thread is cut from thin brass sheet and folded to grip the thread. The knot is tied to join the thread together into a loop and the knot smeared with pva glue to prevent stray ends of thread from snagging the pylons.

BELOW: *Fig. 176   The hill station brass tube support for the freewheeling pulley is bent forwards to align the nylon thread with the pulley groove; the tube support is also bent to adjust the thread tension. A coloured bulb to illuminate the inside of the building is supported on an aluminium tube permitting the building to be removed without trailing connecting wires. A small dummy pylon is mounted behind the pulley wheel with a further pylon painted on the back panel to give the illusion the cable cars continue into the distant landscape. The nylon thread runs on the underside of the piano-wire pylon arms to prevent the car hanging hooks being snagged.*

Fig. 177 The hill station building in position. The slot in the base allows the removal of the building without having to remove the pulley wheel.

THE CABLE CARS AND PYLONS

Styrene sheet is cut out for the roofs and bases of the cable cars, and styrene strip is cut to make the frames for the hook attachments. I have to confess on cheating where constructing the convex windows on the cars is concerned. Generally speaking, windows would normally be cut from clear, flat, acetate sheet and then bent to shape. However, this would be quite fiddly to do on this small size, probably resulting in glue-smudged, poorly fitting joints in an attempt to hold and bend the pieces of acetate together at the same time.

What I required was a rigid, clear plastic, moulded, curved material, which could be just cut to the shape and glued in place – enter the humble discarded clear plastic bottle. This unlikely source

of material provided a couple of suitably moulded, curved sections of plastic, which I cut out and used to construct the car window sides to which the car bases were glued.

N-gauge painted seated figures are glued inside the cars before finally gluing on the roofs. To paint the cars, start by cutting the window shapes from masking tape and sticking them to the car sides, and the corners, bases and roofs painted using acrylic paint.

The pylons are basically posts with a hook on each end of horizontal arms to guide the nylon loop thread between the two pulley wheels. Piano-wire is cut and bent to form the hook guides, and are glued into the top of aluminium tube posts. To enhance the appearance of the pylons, styrene

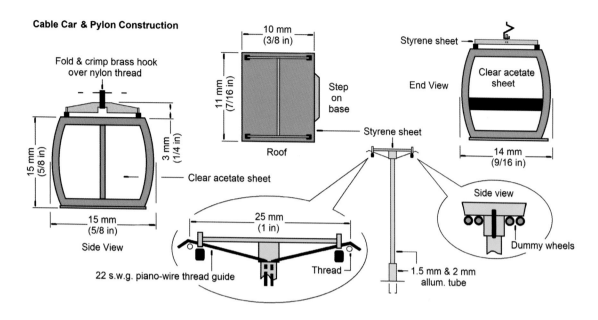

Cable Car & Pylon Construction

Fold & crimp brass hook over nylon thread

15 mm (5/8 in)

15 mm (5/8 in)

Side View

Clear acetate sheet

3 mm (1/4 in)

10 mm (3/8 in)

11 mm (7/16 in)

Step on base

Roof

Styrene sheet

Styrene sheet

End View

Clear acetate sheet

14 mm (9/16 in)

Side view

Dummy wheels

25 mm (1 in)

22 s.w.g. piano-wire thread guide

Thread

1.5 mm & 2 mm allum. tube

Fig. 178 Construction details for one of the two cable cars. The sliding door panel is represented on the side view with a centrally painted vertical strip; this is omitted on the inner face of the cars.

sheet is used to disguise the piano-wire hooks, and dummy guide wheels, cut from plastic rod, are glued to the ends of the pylon arms. The cable cars are attached opposite each other on the nylon thread loop, which is tensioned by bending the brass pulley wheel supporting tube at the hill station so the tops of the car-attachment hooks just clear the underside of the piano-wire thread guides on the pylons.

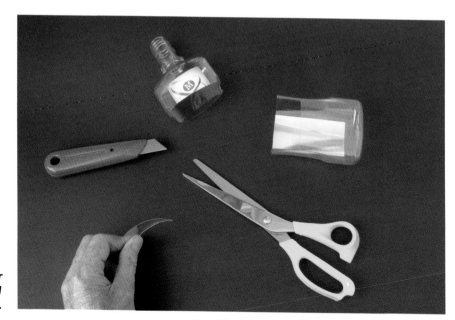

Fig. 179 Discarded clear plastic bottles or plastic packaging can be recycled to provide a source of material for constructing the curved cable-car window sides.

Fig. 180 Window shapes are cut from masking tape when painting the cars.

Fig. 181 Seated N-gauge figures are glued inside the cars before the roofs, with the hook attachment slots, are glued into place.

Fig. 182 To replicate this complex working full-size wheel arrangement, shown here at the recently rebuilt cable car at Dubrovnik, is probably not a practical proposition in N gauge, although dummy wheels could be constructed from plastic rod and styrene for a passable realistic appearance.

CABLE-CAR BASE AND HILL STATION BUILDINGS

These buildings are constructed from scratch using styrene sheets, and are attached to the layout with small screws to enable them to be easily removed for access to the pulley wheels. Clear acetate sheet is used for the windows and for constructing the circular wall on the base station, through which the cable cars can be seen in motion inside. The buildings are painted with acrylic paint, and printed card roof tiles are used for the hill station. N-gauge figures are glued inside the buildings prior to the roofs being permanently attached. The dimensions for the base- and hill-station sides, bases and roofs are plotted on squared paper. They are then cut out to use as templates for the styrene sheet parts. If you wish to construct buildings to your own design, then the only important factor to consider is to allow sufficient clearance for pulley wheels and moving cars within the buildings.

Fig. 183   *N-gauge painted figures inside the base station are glued on to a raised platform, constructed from styrene sheet at the same height as the door steps on the cable cars. The handrail is bent from piano wire and is glued into the raised platform.*

Cable-Car Base Station

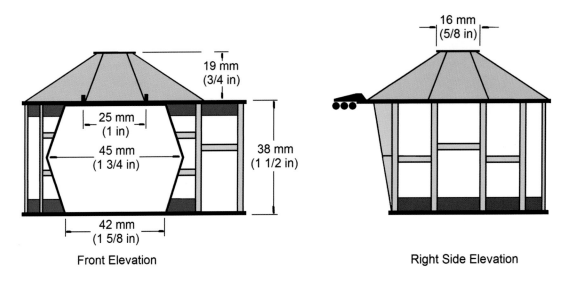

Front Elevation

Right Side Elevation

Fig. 184 *The principal dimensions of the base station. Clear acetate sheet to form the wall of the building is glued to the inside of the framework.*

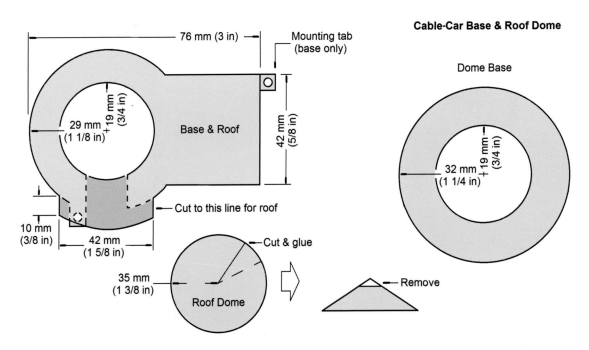

Fig. 185 *The base and roof parts of the base station. The roof dome is cut from thin styrene sheet for bending to shape.*

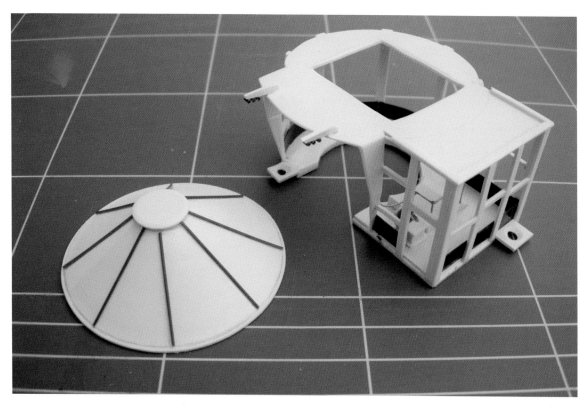

Fig. 186 *Construction of the base station is almost complete. A square access opening was cut into the top of the prototype building, although this can be circular, as shown in Fig. 185. The narrow, black panel, subsequently painted blue, is cut from thin styrene sheet so that it can be bent and glued on the inside of the framework around the base. Plastic rod is used to replicate the segment joints on the roof dome.*

Fig. 187 *This view of the completed hill station shows the position of the window on the left side of the building, which is not shown in Fig. 188. N-gauge figures are glued to a base prior to the roof being fitted.*

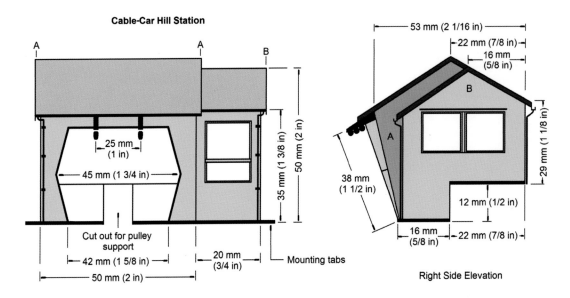

Fig. 188 *The principal dimensions of the hill station. Drain pipes and the dummy guide wheels are made from plastic rod.*

BUILDINGS AND LOCATIONS

Up to this stage in constructing the layout I had not planned on what type of buildings, other than the three stations, would be suitable for hopefully creating interesting focal points. Once again I fired up my computer to see what was available online and, together with browsing through catalogues, quickly discovered that there are plenty of N-scale buildings to choose from. Most of the leading model train manufacturers and suppliers produce buildings and other lineside structures as either readymade painted resin mouldings or plastic kits, including a couple of manufacturers who specialize in card kits.

Readymade, off-the-shelf buildings have the advantage that they can be immediately installed on the layout, and they can also be physically viewed at your local model railway shop to give an idea on how they might fit and look on the layout prior to purchase. Indeed, this is how some of my ideas formed for creating the roads to service the buildings and where I could incorporate green areas on the landscape. Ideally, it would be preferable here

to describe the sequence in installing all buildings on the layout in one go. However, in reality, some of the buildings could be installed on the landscape straightaway, whilst other buildings were installed after completion of the water feature, including on any remaining suitable spaces I could find.

Buildings that are made from plastic kits or are built from scratch arguably offer the most realistic-looking buildings and structures, whereby individual bricks or stones can be picked out and highlighted with different paint shades on the embossed detailed walls provided in some plastic kits. The included down-pipes and gutters also look more authentic where these are glued on separately to buildings. The kits include detailed illustrated assembly instructions for gluing the parts together with a liquid solvent, which usually has to be purchased separately, and the solvent applied with a small brush, sometimes included in the lid of the bottle. Plastic moulding flash, where individual parts are joined to supporting armatures during manufacture, are removed with a sharp knife prior to painting.

Fig. 189   A comprehensive range of N-scale buildings and structures is available to choose from, either online or from catalogues, and include: (1) Ratio and Wills, who specialize in plastic kits of buildings, bridges, semaphore signals and styrene sheets in various embossed brick and stone finishes for making buildings from scratch; (2) Peco, besides being a foremost producer of track and rolling stock, also offer a range of plastic kits of buildings, bridges and tunnel mouths; (3) Graham Farish is a well-established source for N-scale locomotives, rolling stock and other railway-related items, including their Scenecraft range of readymade buildings and structures.

Card kits of buildings and other structures are comprised of pre-cut printed detailed card parts that are simply pressed out from the surrounding sheet, then folded using a straight edge and the parts glued together with a clear adhesive, such as UHU glue. Thick, plain card is usually included in the kits to use where necessary to strengthen some parts. Although details on the card parts are only printed, they nevertheless look convincing at N scale, even when viewed close up and personal.

Card buildings can be further improved by adding guttering and down-pipes using plastic rod, and television aerials made from household fusewire, for example. The buildings are also easily adapted for lighting by cutting away the base and internal card walls to enable bulbs to be fitted.

The completion of all the buildings on the layout resulted in a somewhat eclectic mix of styles ranging from English traditional and modern, Austrian, to a photograph of a Spanish town pasted on to the painted backscene. The buildings are positioned temporarily at first on the layout to see how they will look and this also affords the opportunity to mark the position of roads. The majority

Fig. 190   A selection of Hornby buildings from their Lyddle End range used on Teignside Quay. (Please note, some of these buildings have since been withdrawn from the Lyddle End range, although they may still be available online from auction sites or other model railway retailers.)

Fig. 191   This small readymade toilet building by Graham Farish could also easily be modified to make a lineside hut by cutting off the Gents sign.

of the buildings have been adapted to be internally illuminated. If you intend to illuminate any of the buildings, then bulbs or LEDs should be fitted at this stage with sufficient lengths of dropper connecting wires, as shown for the station buildings in Fig.146. When the buildings are permanently positioned on the layout with screws or glue, it is a good idea to instal the buildings first at the back of the layout and work towards the front to hopefully avoid knocking off the odd chimney pot or two or other tall items when leaning over the layout. Of course, the layout can also be turned around to reach awkward areas. With any moderately large layout, such as Teignside Quay, one has a choice of either installing all the buildings and roads on the entire layout first in one go, then adding the landscaping features, or completing the buildings and all the landscaping, including trees and foliage and such, on just one part of the layout at a time before moving on to the next section. The advantage with this last method is that it is relatively quick to see the final result and also it does enable you hone your landscaping skills.

The locations and suggested numbered sequence in installing the buildings on Teignside Quay are

Fig. 192   A selection of plastic kits of buildings used on Teignside Quay. Faller is a German producer of plastic kits, such as this group of Austrian-style houses. Other producers of buildings include Peco and Ratio.

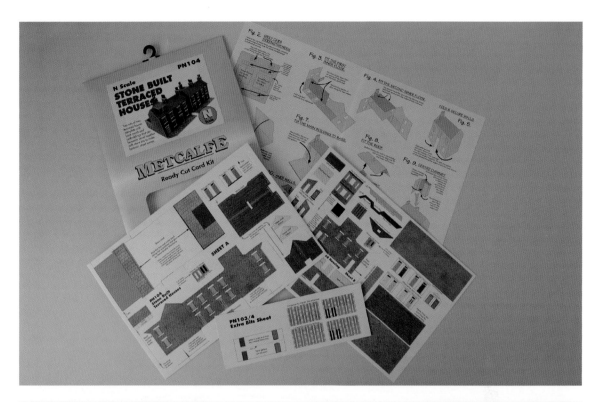

Figs 193 and 194   Metcalfe ready cut card kits include buildings, station platforms, paving, printed brick and stone-patterned paper and card sheets for facing walls.

Fig. 195   The numbered locations of the buildings referred to in the text. Buildings adjacent to the water feature are installed after this feature is completed.

shown in Fig. 195. The locations and details of the buildings, including the surrounding landscape are described. Landscaping materials, such as scatter grass, trees and foliage, used on the layout are produced by Woodland Scenics. Vehicles and figures are by, Busch, Modelscene, Graham Farish, Oxford Diecast, Kato and Wiking, to name a few.

LOCATION NO. 1

This is where the buildings were first installed on the layout after completing the hill sub-structure. Rigid foam is used to build the embankments on each side of the road, which is cut out from card and glued to the sub-structure. Filler is applied to gaps before sprinkling and gluing scatter grass to the hill surface to which trees are inserted.

Fig. 196   Location No. 1: the houses are plastic kits by Faller, one of which is internally illuminated to complement the working street-lights, which are constructed from aluminium tubing. The obelisk is made from balsawood and the road paved with strips of Metcalfe printed brick-effect card. The painted road continues on to the backscene to give the illusion of distance.

Fig. 197   Location No. 1: setting out the positions of the houses using the plastic bases as a guide. The card road base is curved downwards out of view towards the back of the layout to hide the joint with the painted backscene, which will be painted on a removable panel.

Fig. 198   Location No. 2: the Masons Arms public house is from Hornby's Lyddle End range of readymade buildings, while the seated figure is glued to a simple bench made from styrene sheet. Teignside Halt is built from scratch using styrene sheet or card, with handrails constructed from household fusewire.

Fig. 199   Location No. 2: the front of the platform of Teignside Halt is cut to match the track curvature; allow sufficient clearance for long carriages when gluing the platform to the layout.

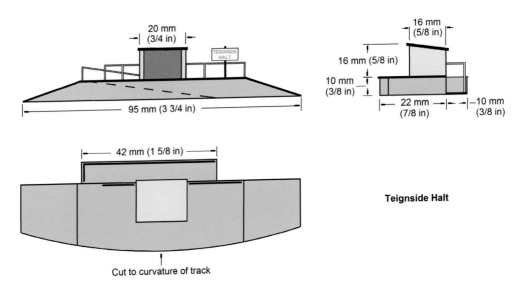

Fig. 200   Overall dimensions for constructing the Halt from styrene sheet or card.

Fig. 201   Location No. 3: Teignside Glen Station building is a Peco plastic kit sitting on a Metcalfe card platform kit, the adjacent signal box is from the Graham Farish range of readymade buildings and the lineside hut is a Ratio plastic kit. The readymade catenary poles are by Kato, the suggested spacing of which are stated on the packaging.

LOCATION NO. 2

This includes a readymade public house and a small station halt constructed from styrene sheet. The public house is set in a slightly elevated position on a rigid foam base facing a small pond. Filler is applied over cork bark for the small rock features, which are painted in shades of brown, white and grey.

LOCATION NOS 3, 4 AND 5

This is Teignside Glen, a night and day scene of a double-track siding in a setting of a terraced row of cottages and a detached house, served by a station with an adjacent signal box and lineside hut. The terrace and detached house are mounted on an embankment, made from rigid foam sheet. The rock-face effect in the background is painted cork bark, glued to the side of the hill sub-structure, and includes a waterfall. The terraced roofs are individually colour washed in different shades of grey to represent new and older slates. Further details include adding a gated wall made from stone printed card, which is glued along the terraced frontages, and a line of washing made from paper, strung with thin wire behind the detached house.

Spare road space at the end of the terrace is taken up with a modern-style garage block, built from scratch using styrene sheet. Working platform lighting is constructed from aluminium tubing, while the crook-style street-light columns are formed by thinly coating epoxy resin over one of the two

Fig. 202 Location No.4: a card kit of a row of terraced cottages and paving stones, both produced by Metcalfe. Cottages were further improved with the addition of a gated card wall and drain pipes made from plastic rod. The detached house with extension is a plastic kit by Peco.

Fig. 203 Location No. 4: household fusewire is used for constructing the television aerial for one of the stone cottages.

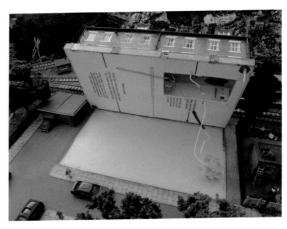

Fig. 204 Location No. 4: up and under view of the card base of the cottages which is cut away for the internal lighting wiring connections; note the screw fastening for easy access.

insulated bulb wires to retain the crook shape of the column. The tram was an afterthought, and probably implausible in the real world when considering the landscape topography. However, as we are in the realms of fantasy here, anything goes on the layout. Tram services start and terminate behind Teignside Glen Station, where readymade catenary poles are glued through the edges of the ballasted track and continue around one of the track circuits. Catenary wires were not fitted as it was considered these would make track cleaning difficult and the wires could easily be damaged. The pantograph arrangement on top of the tram is cosmetic, electrical current to power the tram is picked up via its wheels from the track in a similar way to other types of model railway locomotives.

Fig. 205 Location No. 5: a block of two modern-style garages constructed from styrene sheet.

Garage Block

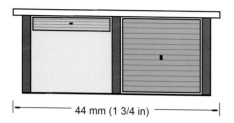

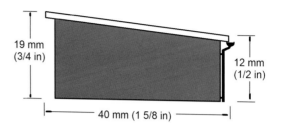

19 mm
(3/4 in)

12 mm
(1/2 in)

44 mm (1 3/4 in)

40 mm (1 5/8 in)

Fig. 206   Overall dimensions for constructing the garages from styrene sheet.

LOCATION NO. 6

This is the crescent-shaped retaining wall, con-structed from card and covering the edge of the elevated, rigid foam sub-structure on which the road leading to the cable car is painted. The arched retaining wall beneath the cable car is a commer-cially available plastic moulding. The arch centres are cut out to show the vehicles travelling through the tunnel, which is internally illuminated with a bulb positioned inside above one of the arch pillars.

Fig. 207   Location No. 6: night scene of the cable car. The arched retaining wall is constructed from the Ratio range of plastic walling and fences, the handrail is constructed from piano wire and glued into the top of the arched wall, which is pre-bent in hot water and is a push fit to allow easy removal.

Fig. 208 The tunnel crash-barrier is made by bending piano-wire and gluing to supports cut from styrene sheet. Fibre-optic cable is used for car lights, glued through pre-drilled holes in the plastic car body.

LOCATION NO. 7

This is Teignside, the mainline station serving the two outer track circuits and positioned alongside the inner-track circuit, bounded by a printed stone-effect card retaining wall covering the side of the rigid foam supports of the elevated track. The top of the wall is capped with a painted notched card strip to represent coping stones. The platforms are constructed in two halves over the layout joint to enable the layout to be folded. Tram services are served by a dedicated track-level platform extension, positioned on the end of the mainline platform and constructed from styrene sheet, although ordinary card could also be used. Adjacent lineside

Fig. 209 Location No. 7: Teignside mainline station, buildings, oil depot, platforms, footbridge, water tower, walls and fencing are plastic kits produced by Ratio. The hut at the back of the tram platform is a Peco kit. The end of the plastic platform is cut to follow the curvature of the track and the platform side bent and glued to the curved edge.

structures include an oil depot, a hut and a water tower. All these items, including the station building and footbridge, are plastic kits and are painted before they are permanently installed on the layout.

The inside of the footbridge and the underside of the station canopy are fitted with bulb lighting, together with the working platform light-columns, constructed from aluminium tubing.

Fig. 210   Oil depot end of Teignside Station with a Peco buffer stop terminating the unpowered track. Loose N-gauge track ballast replaces the moulded plastic ballast on top of the buffer stop. Wooden track-crossing boards are replicated by cutting and scoring styrene sheet, and then painted muddy brown. Wheel clearance between the boards and rails is checked with a locomotive or a wagon before the glue has set. The gravel effect on the ground is sharp sand, which is available from a builders' yard, and is sprinkled on and soaked with pva glue, diluted with grey-coloured water applied with a syringe. Peco cable-laying figures are repainted in current health and safety high-visibility colours.

Fig. 211   Stone-embossed styrene sheet is used to construct the shelter, which is similar in size to the shelter on Teignmouth Halt Station.

Fig. 212 Location No. 8: Teignside Quay Station is a readymade waiting room produced by Hornby, from their Lyddle End range of buildings, and is modified with the addition of a Ratio plastic canopy glued on to the front. The shed is a Peco plastic kit and the platform a Metcalfe card kit. Peco platform seats, Ratio fencing and Graham Farish figures are also used in this scene.

LOCATION NO. 8

This is Teignside Quay Station, located within a fictional preserved railway line setting serving the water-basin feature. The buildings are a mixture of readymade and a plastic kit, with a platform constructed from a card kit.

LOCATION NO. 9

This is a modern-style level-crossing, which is temporarily positioned on the layout together with the station platforms at the track-laying stage. The position of the crossing also determines how roads are to be eventually routed and where the nearby road bridge can be located.

LOCATION NO. 10

This is an imposing readymade resin-moulded manor house set on an elevated position carved from rigid foam overlooking the water basin and mainline station. The house is adapted for internal lighting using bulbs by drilling out the solid resin tower and some of the windows, after first prising away the acetate window frames. These are subsequently detailed with curtains, painted on the

Fig. 213 Location No. 9: the modern-style level-crossing and lineside hut are Peco plastic kits, with warning lights painted on the light display boards; these could be modified to working, flashing lights with miniature LEDs. Wheel clearance is checked between the rails and crossing with a locomotive or a wagon before the crossing is finally glued in place.

Fig. 214   Location No. 10: the manor house is a readymade resin building from the Graham Farish range of buildings and figures. The wedding car is an Oxford Diecast model with white cotton thread glued on the bonnet to represent ribbons. The wedding party are figures produced by the German company, Preiser.

inside of the clear acetate windows. A satellite dish is glued to one of the chimney stacks, and is made from thin styrene sheet clippings using a stationery-type hole punch. The resulting disc clipping is shaped by pressing the rounded blunt end of a pencil on the centre of the disc, supported on a soft surface. The carved-out terraces in the rigid foam are faced with embossed stone-effect styrene sheet walls and paving. Similar embossed sheets are also used to construct the low wall alongside the road verge. The steps leading up to the front of the house, and also at the side of the terrace, are made

Fig. 215   Satellite television dishes are on buildings everywhere nowadays and the manor house is no exception. This satellite dish is made from styrene sheet and fine plastic rod.

Fig. 216   The manor house is mounted on a raised rigid foam sub-structure, carved to shape and the terraces cut out and faced with Ratio embossed stone-effect styrene sheet. The road base is cut from card and glued onto the foam.

Fig. 217   *The solid, moulded resin tower of the manor house is drilled out to accommodate a light bulb and the inside of the building painted to prevent light shining through the resin.*

Fig. 218   *Location No. 11: Ratio manufacture the plastic kit of the Midland-style signal box and the optional interior fittings kit.*

by overlapping and gluing styrene strips together. The gravel-effect driveway and car park at the back of the house are achieved with fine builders' sand, available from builders' merchants, which is sprinkled on the rigid foam and sealed with diluted pva glue, using an eye-drop-type dispenser. In addition to the wedding-party figures and car, other features include fibre-optic lights, fountain made with clear-water effects resin and a helicopter with rotating blades, which was another afterthought, most probably influenced by watching a James Bond film.

LOCATION NO. 11

This is a plastic kit of a Midland-style signal box and is positioned adjacent to the level-crossing. This highly detailed kit is also available with an optional internal fittings kit, which is glued inside. The internal details of the signal box are enhanced by fitting a light bulb concealed in the roof space, as shown in Fig. 150.

LOCATION NO. 12

This features two bungalows in garden settings. One of the bungalows has an armchair, viewed through the window, which is carved from the same type of rigid blue foam used to construct the base of the layout. The density of this foam also makes it ideally suitable for carving small items. A variety of coloured landscaping materials are used to create the grass and foliage. Flowers are made by applying small blobs of coloured acrylic paint to clumps of foam foliage.

Fig. 219 Location No. 12: the roof on the Peco plastic kit bungalow, shown on the left, is removable for access inside, unlike the other bungalow, which is a Hornby resin-moulded building. Garden landscaping materials, such as grass scatter, trees and foliage, are produced by Woodland Scenics; other items include plastic fencing by Ratio and printed card stone walling by Metcalfe.

Fig. 220 Location No. 13: Jordan cork bark is glued over rigid foam to form the rocky outcrop at the far end of the footbridge. The carriage shed and lineside hut are Ratio plastic kits. The red-brick boundary wall between the carriage siding and mainline tracks, including the footbridge supports, are constructed from Metcalfe printed card sheets and road signs are from the Gaugemaster Tiny Signs range.

LOCATION NO. 13

This features a carriage shed, footbridge and a high-ways depot. The footbridge is constructed from styrene sheet and spans all the tracks on this corner of the layout. The footbridge links Teignside Quay Station to the outside world via a row of cottages, a photograph of which is pasted on to a thin plywood panel screwed to the side of the layout. Cork bark is used to create the rocky outcrop on the back of the train controller position, where the far end of the footbridge leads on to a footpath carved into the rigid foam sub-base. The highways depot came about through having a number of road signs left over from completing the roads. This is a typical instance where one aspect generated an idea for another feature on the layout.

LOCATION NO. 14

This is a car-repair garage scene and it was created to fill a gap between the train controller platform and the track. The hill in the foreground is landscaped with grass scatter over a rigid foam sub-structure and the road carved to form a cutting in the Styrofoam baseboard. The garage is internally illuminated and a light bulb is wired to the out-side of the building. A plastic-bodied car was modi-fied by cutting out the bonnet and gluing it in the open position to reveal the engine, made from scrap material and painted black. The car headlights are illuminated using fibre-optic cable, threaded through the baseboard and connected to an LED light source.

Fig. 221   Location No. 14: the embossed styrene stone-effect retaining wall behind the garage, including the fencing, is produced by Ratio, while the garage is a Hornby readymade building. Apart from the tractor, which is from the German company Wiking, the remaining vehicles are from the Oxford Diecast range of vehicles, with the exception of the modified plastic-bodied car, which is by Peco. The gentleman servicing the underside of the car has had his upper body surgically removed (no other plastic figures were harmed in modelling this scene).

Fig. 222   White rigid foam, as used for packaging, is suitable for constructing hill sub-structures such as here at the front of the layout. The embankments are formed with screwed-up newspaper, and held in place with masking tape with pieces of kitchen towel laminated over the top to form a hard shell, as described in the technique shown in Fig. 156. A section of the card road base and the footpath leading to the level-crossing have been cut out and glued to the sub-structure. The tracks partly covering the circular grill is where a loudspeaker is located under the base board for playing recorded railway sounds.

Fig. 223 Location No. 15: the pump house is a Ratio plastic kit set within the backdrop of the Ratio viaduct and the two Peco plate-girder bridges, which are supported on Metcalfe stone-printed card, glued over rigid foam sub-structures. The cable car and roadway retaining wall is made with Ratio embossed stone-effect styrene sheet, colour washed to highlight the individual stones.

LOCATION NO. 15

This features a plastic-kit model of a restored pump-house that may have been used for industrial purposes, or in this case to raise the water level in the adjacent lock. The moulded stones in the walls are highlighted by brushing a white colour wash over the walls and then, when almost dry, the colour wash is rubbed off the surface with a cloth leaving the white mortar effect between the stones.

Some of the remaining buildings and other structures were installed after completion of the river-basin water feature. The description of these additional buildings is included here as Location Nos 16–18.

LOCATION NO. 16

This is a readymade farm building, which is also suitable for use as a boat-repair workshop and is sited at the back of the river-basin feature. The adjacent parasol-covered seating is constructed from styrene sheet. Some of the boats are painted white metal mouldings and are amongst the last items to be included on the layout. The layout joint is noticeable when viewed from above; in particular, where smooth surfaces occur such as on roads. However, the joint is almost invisible when the layout is viewed from a more horizontal perspective, when using legs or a high table to support the layout.

LOCATION NO. 17

Space was found beside the water feature for this readymade stores building and a lifting bridge, constructed using strip and sheet styrene. This part of the layout is floodlit at night with an ultra-bright LED, mounted at the top of a tall aluminium tube column.

Fig. 224   Location No. 16: this Hornby readymade farm outbuilding serves as a boat-repair workshop. Figures and vehicles are from the same suppliers and producers mentioned in the other locations, while the dinghies are white metal mouldings manufactured by Langley Models.

Fig. 225   Location No. 17: the lock-side stores is a Hornby readymade building glued alongside Metcalfe printed card block paving, which surrounds the water feature. Fencing is by Ratio and the lifting bridge is built from scratch, details of which are shown in Fig. 237.

LOCATION NO. 18

This is a kiosk, made using styrene sheet and constructed by wrapping and gluing the styrene sheet counterside to the sides of the circular base and counter top. The diameter of the canopy is cut slightly larger than the counter, and is cut and glued to form the dome shape, in a similar way to making the circular domed roof for the cable-car building in Fig. 185. The canopy is mounted to the counter base using plastic rod or aluminium tube, and balsawood is used to make the square tea-dispensing machine, which is sealed with superglue and then painted.

Fig. 226 Location No. 18: tea is served in white painted mugs made from aluminium tube from this scratch-built kiosk. Road markings are self-adhesive coloured coach lining, available from the Hobby's catalogue. The figure in the blue jacket seems to have forgotten to remove his diving boots but, in reality, I omitted to cut away the plastic moulding flash from his otherwise normal size shoes.

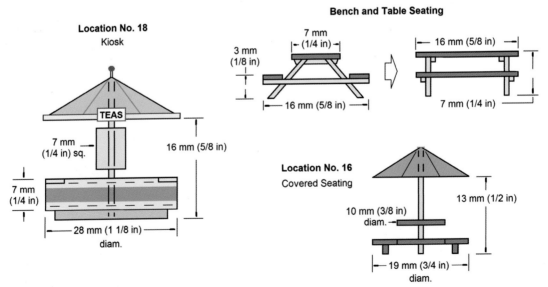

Fig. 227 The principle dimensions of the kiosk and the circular covered seating at Location No. 16. Dimensions and construction details are also shown for the bench tables, which are located by the river basin.

ROADS AND BRIDGES

Road construction was briefly described within the subject of buildings at Location No. 1 (*see* Fig. 197), whereby the road serving the small group of houses was constructed from card and glued to the sub-structure. Art-quality card of approximately 1.5mm (1/16in) thickness is used at this location and also for the elevated roads on either side of the road bridge. The road width at Location No. 1 is drawn on to card 30mm (1 3/16in) wide and is cut slightly wider for gluing the verge landscaping over the card edges. The turning circle is drawn on using a pair of compasses. The card driveway to the parking area is cut slightly wider than a width of a car. Pva adhesive is used to glue the card road to the sub-structure, although contact glue is useful where instant adhesion is required to hold card on undulating terrain, for example.

The double-track road bridge at the front of the layout is constructed from a Peco plastic kit and is painted before gluing the bridge to the baseboard. The position of the bridge dictates the shape of the elevated adjoining roads, which are drawn onto the baseboard, from which the card roads are cut out using tracing paper to transfer the shape of the road onto the card. The card road sections are glued on top of equally spaced rigid-foam supports, glued to the baseboard. This method is also used to construct and mount the adjacent footpath to which the embankment, here, and also on each side of the road, is formed with rigid foam and screwed-up newspaper, and subsequently covered with glued-on laminated layers of kitchen towel to form a hard shell.

Fig. 228   The position of the completed Peco double-track road bridge and shape of the painted card approach roads. The single-carriageway road leading to the station car park is also made from card.

Fig. 229 The bridge deck and card roads are 30mm (1³⁄₁₆in) wide, and the embankments are formed with screwed-up newspaper, held in place with masking tape. The footpath, also made from card, terminates at a rail crossing at the station. The gully water-feature is carved into the foam baseboard and shortened Peco girder bridge sides, including the tunnel mouth, are glued in place prior to creating the remaining embankments.

Fig. 230 The footpath side of the landscaped embankment. Fence posts are painted matchsticks with household fusewire glued on, and the rail crossing is scored and painted styrene sheet to replicate wooden boards.

The section of road running along the back of Teignside Quay Station is raised to the same level as the platform by roughly cutting to shape a sheet of 6mm (¼in) rigid foam, cut to fit against the back of the station platform and to include the level-crossing and also the location of the river-basin feature. It is advisable to remove the station first to avoid potential damage before marking and cutting out the position of the river basin, which is done before the foam sheet is permanently glued to the baseboard. Roads are marked out on the foam, and the edges carved and smoothed to feather into the level of the adjoining roads on the baseboard, which have been painted with two or three coats of matt-grey acrylic paint and lightly sanded to remove any high spots.

The road fronting the row of terraced stone cottages is painted 25mm (1in) wide directly on to the flat, rigid-foam embankment, while the approach road to the cable-car station is painted 30mm (1³⁄₁₆in) wide on to the foam sub-structure.

Grey-coloured roads can be painted on card or Styrofoam by gradually adding small amounts of matt black to a mainly matt-white paint mix until the right shade of grey is obtained. Paint supplied in tins should not be thinned; however, if using artists' acrylic tube paint, this will require thinning with water to resemble a runny treacle-like consistency.

Long tail-chasing trains on tight curves are not an ideal combination to have, as the trains are inclined to look more toy-like than the authentic alignment of carriages in the full-size world. However, where there is a lot of track occupying a relatively small space, such as with the Teignside Quay layout, tight curves are inevitable. One solution here is to run short-length trains, or trains with short-wheelbase

Fig. 231 The road behind the station and the roads around the roundabout are painted 30mm (1³⁄₁₆in) wide onto the foam sub-structure, which is first sealed by brushing with diluted pva glue.

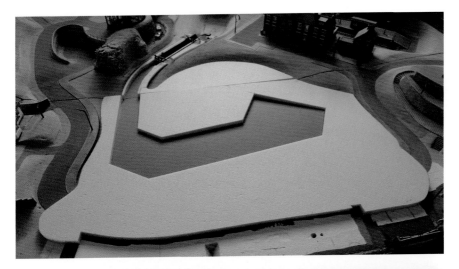

Fig. 232 Teignside Quay Station is removed and the shape of the river basin, shown in Fig. 240, is cut out from 6mm (¼in) Styrofoam and is glued to the top of the baseboard.

Fig. 233 The roads are drawn on and the edges of the foam sheet are carved and feathered into the adjacent painted-on roads. The pavement height at the back of the station is built up to the same level as the platform using card that is glued to the foam sheet.

Fig. 234 Location of the footbridge, which is built from scratch using styrene sheet and plastic rod. Planting trees, as well as installing the bridge, helps to reduce the impact of curved tracks.

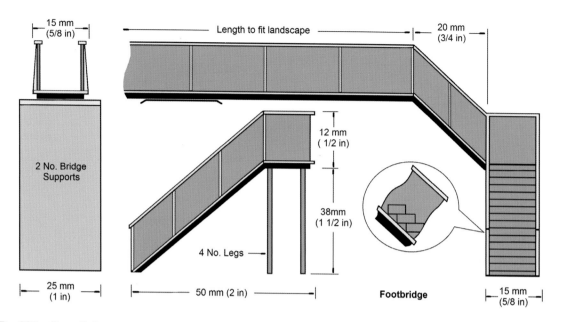

Fig. 235 *Overall dimensions and construction details of the footbridge, the length of which is made to fit between the landscaped train controller position and Teignside Quay Station.*

Fig. 236 *The hand-cranked pedestrian lifting bridge is glued to the Metcalfe printed stone-effect card paving. The figure and buggy are by Graham Farish.*

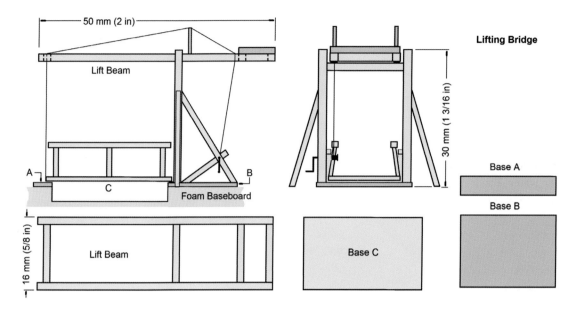

Fig. 237   Overall dimensions of the lifting bridge to span a 25mm (1in) wide water feature, constructed from either styrene sheet and strip or from stained balsawood.

rolling stock, such as freight wagons, for example. The appearance of tight curves can, in some degree, be minimized by disguising them with strategically placed buildings or trees alongside the track. Apart from installing tunnels, another ploy is to place a bridge over the curved track, which I have done here by installing a long footbridge over the five curved tracks in front of the train controller.

The footbridge in question is constructed from styrene sheet, including the steps, which are made by gluing overlapping strips of styrene together. Plastic rod is used to construct the supporting pillars. The bridge-supporting walls are constructed from balsawood and the curved wall alongside the track is made from card, both of which are covered with printed brick-effect paper.

A small lifting bridge will add character to the layout and is glued in place when the water feature and surrounding printed-card paving effect is completed. The hand-cranked pedestrian bridge is representative of its full-size counterpart of the type of bridge still in use in some parts of the UK. The bridge can be constructed in either the raised or lowered position.

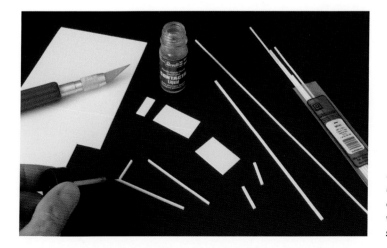

Fig. 238   Styrene strips and sheet are used to construct the frame members and the deck of the lifting bridge, which is glued together with plastic solvent applied with a brush.

WATER FEATURES

There are several methods for creating realistic water features. One method is to cut out the shape of the intended water feature from clear, rigid acetate or polyester sheet. This is then painted on the underside with a light-grey/brown colour around the periphery of the sheet and brushing a darker shade of colour towards the centre to represent deeper water. Landscaping materials, such as grass scatter and green-coloured foam foliage, are then glued around the outside to hide and cover the edges between the sheet and the existing landscape. Another method is to paint card or styrene sheet a pond or river colour and apply several coats of clear varnish on top.

For the water features on Teignside Quay, I decided to try using a clear-setting resin that is poured straight from the bottle. The river-basin feature, and the river flowing from it, which disappears under the viaduct, are constructed in six separate modular sections, including the lock, to

Fig. 239   To create the water effect, clear-setting resin, produced by Woodland Scenics, is poured on to the base of river basin. Masking tape is temporarily taped across the open river end of the base to prevent the resin from escaping. The mooring posts and basin sides are constructed from balsawood and are covered with Metcalfe stone-effect printed card and Ratio stone-embossed styrene.

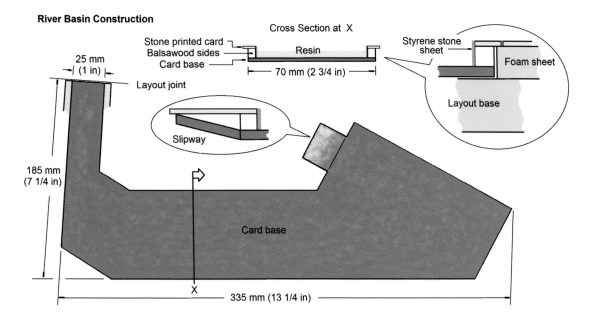

Fig. 240   Art-quality card is used for the base of the river basin; the dimensions shown are for guidance – the shape and size can be altered, if required.

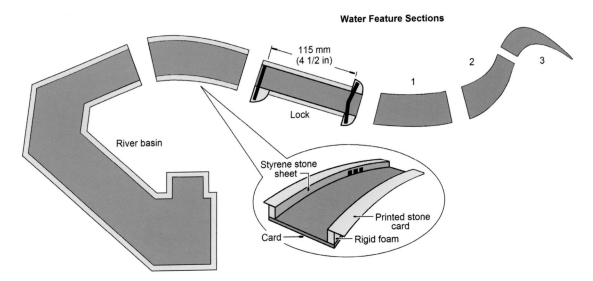

Fig. 241   The lock used on the layout is a Hornby readymade item that has been reduced in length by cutting out a section in the middle and rejoining the two ends together. Sections 1, 2 and 3, are cut from card, which is painted and coated with several layers of clear resin, applied with a brush.

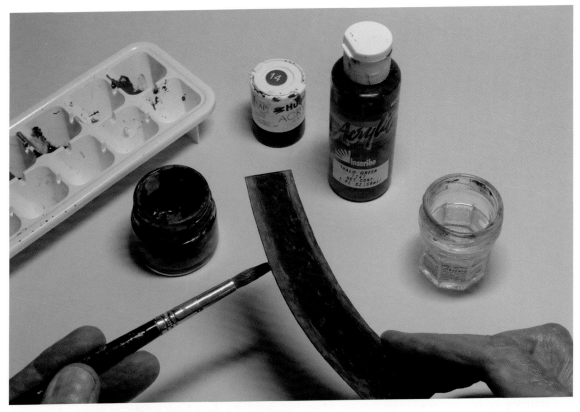

Fig. 242   Painting the underside of clear polyester sheet is another method of creating water effects.

avoid attempting to pour the resin in one go into one continuous length of carved-out riverbed. Basically, the individual sections of the water feature are shallow trays into which the resin is poured. This is done on a table that must be flat. When the resin has set, the sections are joined together and glued into a carved-out channel in the baseboard of the layout.

The river basin is the first section to be constructed. Card is used for the base and the shape cut out to fit in the recess in the rigid-foam sheet on the layout, as shown in Figs 232 and 233. The sides are cut from balsawood and are glued around the top edges of the base. Pva glue is used to seal the card base and balsawood sides prior to gluing on stone-effect styrene sheet around the inside to represent the walls. The base and walls are painted a dark-grey/blue colour and the open joint at the river end of the

basin is temporarily closed off and sealed with tape, while clear-setting resin is gently poured to a depth of around 3mm (⅛in) on top of the card base.

Before permanently gluing the river basin in place, the lock, which is a commercially readymade item, is glued into a carved-out channel in the foam baseboard of the layout, checking that it will level correctly with the adjoining river sections when they are glued in place. The curved river section between the basin and the lock is constructed in the same way as the river basin, except the sides are cut from rigid foam. The shapes of the remaining river sections are cut from card and painted a river colour, upon which several layers of clear resin are applied. As an aside here, painted clear acetate or polyester sheet can be used as an alternative material for constructing the basin and river sections. Pva or solvent-free contact adhesive is suitable for

Fig. 243 This completed lock scene shows the raised water-level in the lock, which is achieved by constructing a false bottom from clear resin-coated painted card, supported on rigid foam blocks and glued to the base of the lock.

Fig. 244   An early stage in construction – the lock has just been glued into the carved-out river channel in the foam baseboard and filler has been applied to blend the lock into the surrounding sub-structure. When dry, the filler is smoothed with glasspaper. Gaps between the sides of the river section and the joint with the lock are filled with clear, mouldable water-effects resin gel, produced by Woodland Scenics. The green areas, which have been painted with household emulsion paint, denote where the planned trees and grass landscaping will eventually be located.

Fig. 245   Upstream view of the completed lock scene. Ripple effects on the water and the wash from the lock gates are created by dabbing clear, mouldable, resin gel with a brush onto the surface of the water and highlighting the ripples with white paint using a fairly dry brush.

fixing the river sections and basin to the layout. The river sections are levelled and bedded into the channelled-out foam baseboard using acrylic filler. Joints between the sections are filled in with a clear mouldable resin gel applied with a blunt knife. The resin gel is, in fact, white in colour when it is first squeezed from the bottle, but it dries clear after a few hours. Ripple effects and the wash from the lock gates are created by lightly dabbing the resin gel with a brush onto the dried water-effect surfaces.

The carved-out culvert in the foam baseboard at the front of the layout is first sealed with pva glue and then painted in shades of grey and brown. Several layers of clear resin are dribbled into the channel and each layer allowed to set before adding further layers until the required depth is achieved.

Clear resin is also used in creating the pond in front of the public house, which is made by making a depression with your thumb in the surface of the foam sub-structure. This is then sealed and painted before the depression is filled with resin and landscaping foliage is partly added around the edge of the pond.

The waterfall behind the back of Teignside Tram Link platform is formed by brushing mouldable, clear resin gel into a carved-out channel in the surface of the cork bark rock-face. The bottom of the waterfall, which has nowhere to go, is conveniently hidden from view by a low stone wall along the back of the platform.

Fig. 246   The completed, carved-out, sealed and painted culvert at the front of the layout is filled with the clear resin for the water effect, only applied where the culvert is visible.

Fig. 247 This nature pond outside the public house is another example where clear resin is used for a water effect. One of the pub customers seems a little worse for wear.

Fig. 248 Woodland Scenics mouldable gel is used to create the waterfall using a brush at the back of the Teignside Tram Link platform. The low wall is constructed from Ratio stone-embossed styrene sheet.

GREEN AREAS

These apply to areas of the layout that are predominantly covered by grass or trees, although I had a rough idea which areas were to be grassed over, such as hills, embankments and verges. However, the positioning of trees requires some thought, especially on the top of hills, in relation to being able to close the folding layout. Armed with a pot of matt-green paint – household emulsion is suitable – I painted the areas where I planned to use grass scatter and foliage material, and subsequently where trees would eventually be planted. Moreover, painting a liberal coat of emulsion on these areas helps to seal and strengthen the surface of the foam sub-structures to provide a firm foundation for gluing in trees.

Small rocky outcrops within the green areas are formed with household filler and sculpted into rock formations using a blunt knife, before the filler completely dries. Filler is also used to blend together pieces of cork bark in constructing rock-face effects.

Neat pva glue is brushed on the areas that are to be grassed over, working in small areas at a time to avoid the glue beginning to dry. Grass-scatter material is sprinkled evenly on the glue and lightly patted down to assist it being absorbed by the glue. Excess grass scatter is vacuumed away

Fig. 249   The sub-base is painted green to determine which areas are to be covered with grass scatter and trees. Rocky outcrops are created with pieces of cork bark and household filler sculpted with a blunt knife.

Fig. 250   Pva glue is brushed onto the sub-base for areas where grass scatter will be used.

Fig. 251   Woodland Scenics' blended turf grass scatter is sprinkled over the glue and the excess vacuumed away when dry. Two or three layers of different types of grass scatter can be applied in creating short or longer grass effects.

Fig. 252   Foliage, bushes and grass scatter are sealed in place with diluted pva glue, sprayed on using a disused spray dispenser. For safety reasons, any pre-existing labelling on dispenser bottles should be removed.

when the glue has dried. Further grass scatter will probably be required to fill in any bald spots, and also to create different shades, or coarse patches of grass using other scatter materials.

The majority of grass-scatter and foliage products are made from clumps of foam or foam granules, and therefore easily damaged if they are not protected.

Products are available in the form of aerosol-sealing agents, which are sprayed on to foliage and grass scatter to provide a protective seal. However, for those of us who may be on a limited budget, a cost-effective alternative, which works just as well, is to use an empty container with a spray attachment, such as a used nasal-spray bottle, filled with diluted pva glue. Track rails will need to be protected from any wandering spray by covering them with masking tape.

Trees on the layout are an assortment of ready-made and those made from commercially produced plastic tree armatures, available in packs of various sizes and species. The plastic branch armatures are bent to form tree shapes and a tacky setting adhesive brushed on to the branches. The plastic armatures are then dipped into a bowl containing clumps of foam foliage, resulting in a completed tree. Hairspray is used to seal the foliage and the trees left to dry standing on the supplied tree bases, which are removed prior to planting the trees into the landscape with either pva glue or solvent-free contact adhesive.

Hedges and stone walls are also commercially available in rigid strip form, or supplied in rolls of

Fig. 253   A selection of Woodland Scenics plastic tree armatures are bent to the shape of trees. The tacky adhesive used to attach foliage to the armatures has a brush applicator in the lid. Hairspray is used to seal foliage on the tree armatures.

foliage-covered pliable foam, which is cut to length and glued to the landscape. The off-the-roll form of hedging is used on the layout, together with granite chippings-covered foam, representing stone walling. Both the hedging and stone walling are improved by adding coarse grass scatter and applying small dabs of coloured paint to represent gorse and weeds, as shown in Fig. 196.

Gardens outside the two bungalows in Fig. 219 are created with long strands of grass-effect material and grass scatter, using dabs of paint for the flowers and real grains of gravel for the ornamental rocks.

Fig. 254   Making instant trees by dipping glue-coated tree armatures into a bowl of foam foliage is a simple fun way to introduce the younger generation to the joys of railway modelling.

Fig. 255   The retaining wall in this scene is constructed from Metcalfe stone-effect printed card with rock effects created using cork bark and filler. Blended grass-scatter is used on the ground with clumps of foam for bushes and tree foliage. Lineside fencing is a Ratio plastic kit.

CHAPTER SEVEN

BACK AND SIDE SCENES

Essentially, the layout is now completed, although I have heard it said that a layout is never really finished. I think this could possibly be true in respect of finding a corner or two to populate with more figures and vehicles, if subsequently lucky enough to receive these as presents. Arguably, most layouts will benefit from the addition of a scenic background, be it a photograph, print or a painted scene positioned vertically at the edge of the layout. The main purpose of a scenic background is to give the illusion that the landscaping continues on into the distance and does not abruptly stop at the end of the layout, and also to hide that steaming mug of coffee on the adjacent workbench, which otherwise would somewhat spoil the illusion without a scenic background to shut out the real world.

I will describe here two methods of constructing the backscene panels. The first method, and the one used on Teignside Quay, is constructed from hardboard and incorporates folding side-wings for painting on a semi-wrap-around mountainous scene. Corner joints between the folding side-wings and the back panel are semi-concealed, so they are less visible when the layout is viewed from the front. The height of the back panel includes and covers the entire inside back of the layout, thus avoiding a visible joint with the top of the layout back.

CONSTRUCTION SEQUENCE

BACKSCENE PANEL

To obtain the shape of the landscape contour, a straight line is marked on paper the width of the layout; the back of wallpaper is suitable for this. The top-inside edge of the back of the layout is divided with equally spaced spot marks approximately 170mm (6¾in) apart. These marks are repeated along the drawn line on the paper. Measure the distance down at right angles from each spot mark on the back of the layout to the top of the landscape and transfer and mark these measurements on to the paper. The paper can then be cut out to the shape of the contours and used as a template for cutting out the backscene panel and the side wings from hardboard. To strengthen the backscene

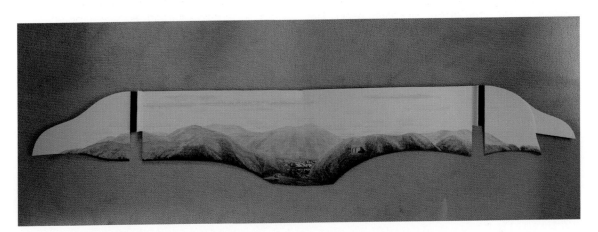

Fig. 256   The folding semi-wrap-around backscene panel slots into the back of the layout, and the side wings fold back for storage.

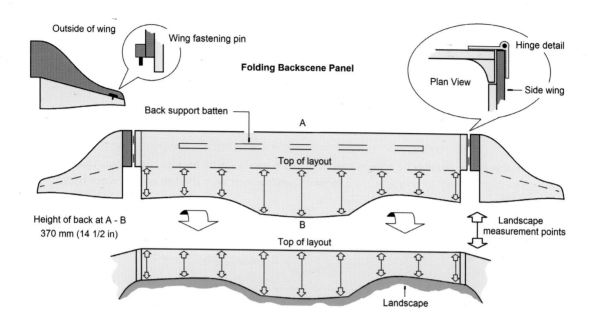

Fig. 257 *Hardboard or plywood is suitable for constructing the folding backscene panel. The arrows indicate where measurements are taken to transfer the shape of the landscape from the layout on to the backscene panel.*

panel, a length of suitably sized timber battening is glued and screwed to the back. The screw heads are sufficiently countersunk for filler to be applied to form a flush surface for painting on the backscene. With the backscene in position, mark and cut out the positions where the 30mm (1¼in) concave-shaped wood mouldings for the corners are screwed to each end of the backscene panel. The mouldings should form a smooth alignment with the top of the existing corner mouldings on the layout.

Folding Side Wings

These are constructed with two glued-together hardboard laminations. The outer lamination is cut so its bottom edge sits on top of the side of the layout, whilst the inner lamination is cut so its bottom edge rests on top of the landscape. Small pins to hold the side wings in position, which slot into pre-drilled holes in top of the layout, are cut from piano wire and glued into wood blocks, which in turn are glued to the outer bottom edge of the side wings. Hinges are screwed to the backscene

panel to which the side wings are screwed, and this enables the wings to fold back for storage. Velcro strips hold the folded wings in place. Stained varnish is applied to the back of the panel and side wings to match the finish of the layout carcass. Two coats of household white primer paint are applied to the faces of the panels, which are rubbed down between coats to ensure a smooth surface upon which to paint the backscene.

SIDE-SCENE PANELS

As the size of the layout is almost as deep as it is wide, the opportunity was taken to include either a painted or a photographic scene on each side of the layout in an attempt to give the illusion of distance. Two matching panels are constructed from 3mm (⅛in) plywood, one for each side of the layout, and are made to slot in between the landscaping and the layout sides. The panels extend the length of both sides of the front half of the layout and are secured to the layout sides with small countersunk woodscrews, with a thin card strip glued along the top

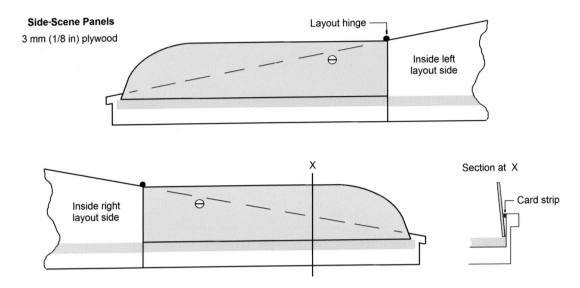

Fig. 258 *The inside faces of the side-scene panels are treated with wood primer before scenic photographs are glued on; stained varnish is applied to the outer surfaces to match the stained finish on the layout.*

edge to angle the panels slightly inwards so as not to obstruct the landscaping when the layout is folded; although, if they do obstruct the landscape, this is fairly easily remedied by cutting a slot along the top of the landscaping to accommodate the top edge of the panels. The edge of the slot can be disguised with small rock outcrops and foliage.

THE LAYOUT PROTECTION PANEL

Another method of providing a backscene is to utilize the layout protection panel, which is normally used to protect the folded layout. Although this option lacks the refinement of the folding side-wings employed on the bespoke backscene panel, it does nevertheless offer a quick and viable alternative in providing a firm foundation on which to mount a scenic print or painting. All that is required to mount the panel on to the back of the layout is 10g. piano wire, cut into three 76mm (3in) lengths to make the panel locating pins. These then slot into pre-drilled holes in the back of the layout, with corresponding holes drilled into the ends of the existing panel support battens to accommodate the other

end of the pins. The pins are a push fit, so they can easily be removed for folding the layout. The two diagonal panel-support bracings are also cut from 10g. piano wire to approximately 470mm (18½in) each in length and the ends bent at right angles to slot into pre-drilled holes in each end of the panel and in the sides of the layout. When the layout is required to be folded, the pins and panel bracing are removed and the panel returned to normal duties by protecting the open side of the folded layout.

CREATING SCENIC PICTURES

HAND PAINTING

I certainly do not consider myself to be at all artistic where splashing paint on canvas is concerned; however, I do see the benefit in painting one's own scenic picture, as it can be tailor-made to suit the layout landscape. For Teignside Quay, I chose to paint a relatively simple mountain scene on to the backscene panel. My first task, after ensuring that

Alternative Back-Panel Arrangement

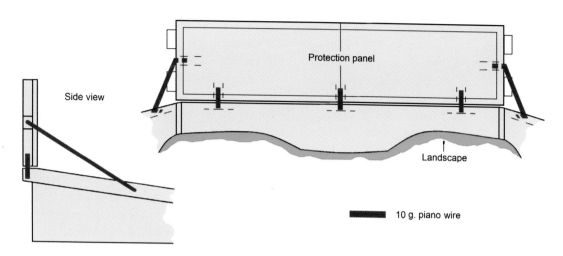

ABOVE: **Fig. 259**   *A card-mounted scenic painting or print is measured and cut to cover the gap between the top of the layout and the protection panel. Blu-Tack is used to mount a scene to the panel.*

BELOW: **Fig. 260**   *Mountains on the folding backscene panel are colour washed using a fairly large, soft bristle brush. Several light colour-washed layers are applied and allowed to dry between washes until the required result is achieved.*

the panel surfaces were smooth and blemish-free, was to paint the face of the backscene panel and folding side-wings a sky-blue colour. By chance, I still had a tin of Dulux sky-blue matt emulsion left over from painting the underside of the foam baseboard. The emulsion is applied using a wide brush, spreading the paint in alternate directions to reduce brush marks, although a paint roller will also produce a smooth finish. The next step is to faintly sketch on the outlines of the mountains with the backscene panel in position, to determine how the mountains and valley contours can be painted when viewed from the viaduct. I had originally intended to paint a town scene in the distant valley. However, I decided to cheat a little, and instead, glued on a photograph of a Spanish town, cut from a magazine, with the edges of the photograph painted to blend in with the surroundings. The mountains are painted on using acrylic paint and thinned with water to make

colour washes of mainly white, green and grey. A pale colour wash is first applied to the distant mountain in the background and stronger shades of colour washes applied to the mountains in the foreground. The conifer trees in the foreground are stippled on using a stiff bristle brush. Additional photographs of buildings are also included on the bottom of the backscene and where buildings can be viewed through the viaduct arches.

USING PHOTOGRAPHS

I have already mentioned using some photographs to compliment the backscene; however, the side-panel scenes are entirely created using photographs.

The side panel behind the main station is covered with two adjoining photographs showing the backs of terraced cottages. These back views are, in fact, photographs taken of the terraced cottages on the layout before the cottages were permanently

Figs 261 (above) and 262 (top of next page)   Photographs of the terraced cottages and row of houses are glued to the side panels, after first printing the photographs out at various sizes on a photocopier to obtain the correct scale and perspective in relation to adjacent buildings and other features on the layout.

installed. The photographs of the cottages are cut out and glued to the side panel. Distant hills are painted on, and pieces of foam foliage glued to the photographs to hide unsightly edges.

The side panel behind the train shed and council depot is covered by a glued-on holiday snap of a row of houses. The council depot approach road is painted on the photograph to give the illusion of perspective, and foam foliage glued to the foreground behind the stone wall where the base of the panel meets the layout.

PRINTED SCENES

These are commercially produced artworks of pre-printed scenes, ranging from hills, mountains and lakes, to dock scenes and townscapes. The scenes can be pasted directly on to a backscene panel or on to a separate card backing. This is particularly useful if you decide to use the layout protection panel for supporting a card-backed pre-printed scene to hide the joint between the panel and the

top of the layout. The card-backed scene, or a hand-painted scene for that matter, is cut to the shape of the landscape, using the same marking-out method described for constructing the backscene panel.

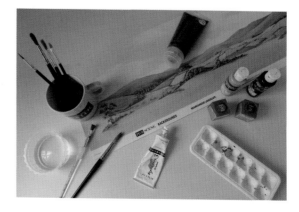

Fig. 263   Peco and Gaugemaster produce a variety of pre-printed scenic backgrounds for pasting on to panels. Artists' acrylic paint, as used on Teignside Quay, is ideal for hand-painting scenic backgrounds.

CHAPTER EIGHT

ADDITIONAL FEATURES

CHILDREN'S ROUNDABOUT

One of the many comments I received during the construction of the layout was a request for a children's roundabout, which I had not originally planned for when scribbling down ideas at the design stage. So, to comply with my family's request, and I also thought it would be a fun feature to have within a possible playground setting, my next task was to decide on how to power the roundabout. To a certain

extent the choice of drive method dictated where the roundabout could be located, as did finding a suitable flat surface to instal it on an increasingly crowded layout. One option was to use a separate dedicated geared electric motor, which would allow a certain amount of freedom as to where to locate the roundabout. However, upon looking at the cable-car gearbox, it was possible to instal a pulley and rubber drive-belt arrangement between the protruding end of the cable-car gearbox shaft and the

Fig. 264 The base of the roundabout is a 50mm (2in) disc, cut from styrene sheet to which a screw-type collar, available from the Hobby's catalogue, is glued to the centre for attaching the roundabout to a brass-tube axle shaft. The collar is disguised by a central reflective beacon feature constructed from plastic off-cuts. A styrene stone-effect wall hides the edge of the roundabout. Playground figures and items, including the miniature ride-on train, are from a Faller plastic kit.

roundabout. This arrangement, though, would have occupied more space under the layout, and the belt drive would not be as positive compared with, say, using bevel gears and a connecting drive shaft, which was my preferred option. The rotation speed of the roundabout can also be varied using the same spare speed control on the train controller that controls the cable car and vehicle turntable. The location of the roundabout is shown in Fig. 83 and shows the route of the drive shaft from the cable-car gearbox.

Clearance has to be allowed for when fitting small bevel gears to be used, on each end of the drive shaft, to determine exactly where to position the roundabout. The base of the roundabout is cut from styrene sheet and a collar with a screw (the type used to retain model aircraft undercarriage wheels

Fig. 265 The bevel gears used to drive the roundabout, available from Maplin Electronics, are a push fit on to the brass-tube roundabout axle and drive shaft. Alternative screw-on type bevel gears are available from the Hobby's catalogue. A plywood or balsawood pad is screwed to the underside of the foam baseboard to support the brass-tube roundabout axle shaft, brass-tube bearing and bevel gear. Screws with attached washers hold the brass-tube drive-shaft support bearings to the timber framework.

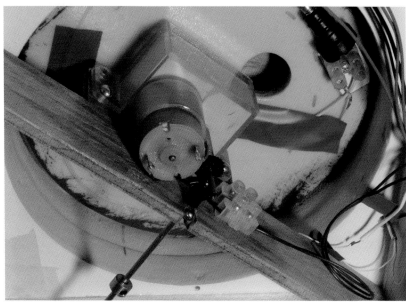

Fig. 266 Brass tubing of the same inside diameter as the gearbox shaft is glued on to form an extension shaft for attaching a bevel gear to drive a children's roundabout.

on axles) is glued to the centre of the roundabout base. This enables the roundabout to be screwed onto an axle shaft, cut from brass tube, which rotates in a support bearing, also cut from brass tube and is glued into a pre-drilled plywood pad for mounting the roundabout bearing with screws to the underside of the layout. A small bevel gear is attached to the bottom end of the roundabout axle-shaft with matching bevel gears attached on to each end of a brass-tube drive-shaft, which connects the roundabout to the cable-car gearbox. A short length of brass tubing is cut and glued to the cable-car gearbox shaft to form a shaft extension on to which a further matching bevel gear is attached. The drive shaft is supported along its length with brass-tube bearings, which are fastened with screws into pre-cut slots in the layout timber-frame members.

Playground furniture items are constructed from a plastic kit, including the ride-on train, which is glued to the base of the roundabout. The remaining playground items, comprising of a swing, see-saw and climbing frames, etc., are glued on to a painted area forming the playground, which is bounded by plastic fencing.

HELICOPTER

In typical 'James Bond' style, a helicopter awaits to whisk away the newly married couple. Perhaps we can only dream of such an occasion. However, in the world of models our dreams can be realized, albeit in miniature.

The wedding scene in the grounds of the manor house is a suitable location for a small helicopter with

Fig. 267 *Your carriage awaits with this modern-equivalent helicopter. The LED is adapted to form the painted fuselage and clear, glazed cockpit, which is illuminated for night duties by wiring the LED with a resistor into the motor circuit.*

motorized rotating rotor blades. Unfortunately, the helicopter does not fly; this certainly would be pushing my model engineering capabilities much too far in N scale. Here, the helicopter is firmly grounded and is constructed using a clear LED to form the basis of the fuselage and cockpit canopy, with the tail boom and free spinning tail rotor blades constructed from fine-bore aluminium tube and styrene sheet. The rotor blade shaft housing on top of the fuselage is carved from balsawood and the main rotor blades are also cut from styrene sheet. Undercarriage skids are cut and bent to shape from household fusewire. Almost any small 3 to 12V electric motor is suitable to spin the main rotor blades. The motor is screwed directly to the underside of the baseboard with the motor shaft joined to a thin piano-wire shaft extension, up through the foam sub-structure of the layout using a short length of glued-on brass tubing packed with balsawood to join the piano wire to the motor shaft. The top end of the piano wire is inserted up through a small pre-drilled hole in the fuselage and the rotor blade

shaft housing (superglue is dripped into the hole in the rotor shaft housing to form a hard-bearing surface prior to inserting the piano-wire extension shaft). A small hole is drilled in the middle of the rotor blades, which are superglued to the extension shaft. Electrical power to the motor is supplied

Fig. 268 *A sensitive, slow-revolution electric motor of up to 12V, which powers the helicopter rotor blades, is fastened to the underside of the foam baseboard with pva glue-coated screws.*

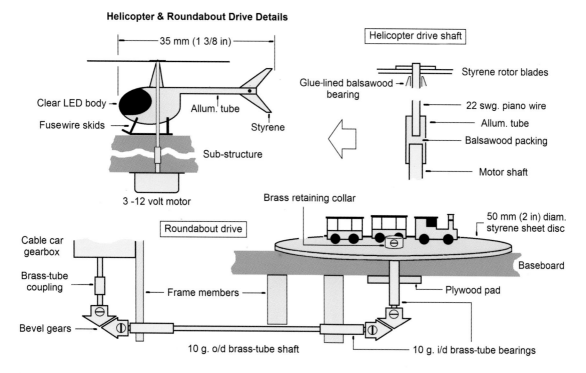

Fig. 269 *The helicopter and roundabout drive details.*

through the same circuit that powers the cable car via the spare speed control on the train controller. An isolating switch is wired into the circuit so that the helicopter motor can be turned on or off independently of the cable car.

SOUND BITES

Station announcements and engine sounds will add realism to the layout operation, and while a digital command control (DCC) layout can support locomotives with engine sounds already built in, an analogue layout such as Teignside Quay can be similarly endowed with sound features. One or two manufacturers offer hand-held units that are basically a selection of pre-recorded train sounds that are independently selected by the push of a button. A similar result can be achieved by downloading and recording train sounds from the internet, subject to any copyright restrictions. For Teignside Quay though, I chose to undertake some pleasurable excursions to a heritage railway and to local train stations to record some engine sounds and station announcements using a tape-recorder, although a digital recorder would also be suitable. Not satis-

fied with just playing back a recorded engine sound every time a train on the layout passed by, I discovered online some single-chip storage voice modules that were available. The modules are capable of recording and playing back individual sounds of up to 20sec on pressing the appropriate incorporated micro-switch on each module. A single dedicated sound module for the station announcements and two further modules for engine sounds are each wired to a loudspeaker mounted under the layout and a hole cut out for the speaker in the foam baseboard where the engine sound or voice is required. The three modules are mounted together in a commercially available project box, positioned next to the train controller switch panel, with small holes drilled in the lid of the box to access the playback micro-switch on each module. The recorded sound on the tape-recorder is played on to a microphone included within each module.

VEHICLES, BOATS AND AN AEROPLANE

No self-respecting model railway is complete without at least one or two vehicles to complement

Fig. 270 Sound modules produced by Quasar Electronics are housed in a Maplin Electronics plastic project box, which is a push fit in a cut-out section of the train controller platform. Small holes are drilled in the box lid to operate the playback switches.

Fig. 271   Under the lid, three sound modules are supported on balsawood bearers glued to the box sides. The recording and playback micro-switches are located on the left of the modules with the microphones on the right. Sound output to the loudspeakers is regulated by the two rotary volume controls.

Fig. 272   Recorded station announcements are wired from one of the sound modules to a 76mm (3in) loudspeaker mounted under Teignside Station, through a hole cut in the foam baseboard. A hole is also cut out in the station platform to let the sound through into the station building.

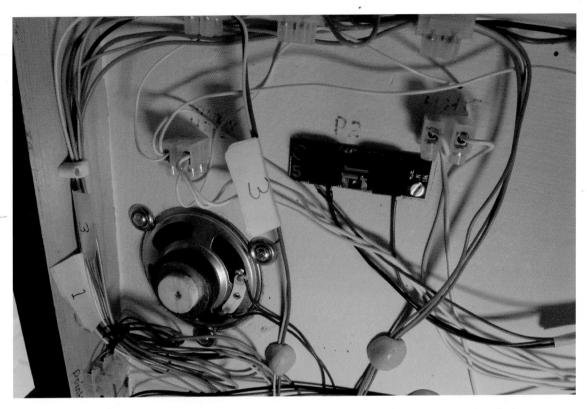

Fig. 273   The loudspeakers for the station announcements, diesel- and steam-engine sounds, which are mounted elsewhere on the layout, are fastened under the foam baseboard with pva glue-tipped screws and cup washers. Blu-Tack is used to secure the wiring to the underside of the foam baseboard.

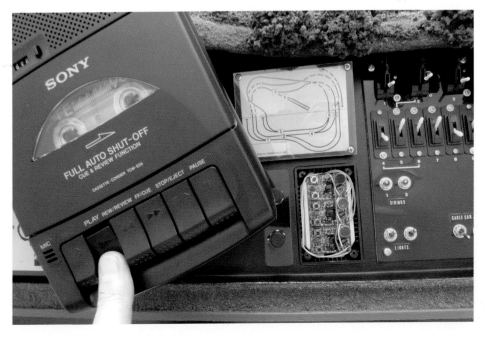

Fig. 274   A tape-recorder is used to play sounds on to the voice/sound modules, which are powered by a separately regulated 5V DC supply from the mains.

a country landscape, and certainly some vehicles are required in a town or a village scene, for example. As for boats, this depends on the type of layout. A dock or harbour scene will probably have commercial and pleasure craft. Aircraft on the other hand have limited applications on a layout, other than perhaps an airport served by a railway. However, as the rule book went out the window a long time ago with Teignside Quay, I have included most forms of transportation on the layout, including cars, vans, a bus, paddle-boarders, boats and even a vintage aircraft.

VEHICLES

N-gauge cars and other vehicles are commercially available in either plastic or metal. The plastic-bodied varieties are usually economically priced and they are fairly easy to customize using a knife or razor saw. An example of a customized car is shown

in Fig. 221, whereby the car bonnet has been cut out and glued in the open position.

Altering the setting of the front-wheel steering to show the wheels set in a turning position will add realism for when a vehicle is positioned on the layout, coming out of a road junction, for example. This modification is made on vehicles where the wheels are attached on steel axles. The first step is to remove the body from the chassis by either removing a small screw or, in the case of plastic bodies, by unclipping and prising off the body with a blunt-pointed knife. Next, remove the front axle by twisting and pulling off one of the front wheels, using a pair of pointed pliers while holding the axle steady with another pair of pliers. The axle is withdrawn from the chassis and the remaining wheel is removed in the same way using pliers. The steel axle is replaced with a copper-wire axle to which the front wheels are reattached. The front wheels

Fig. 275   To make vehicles appear that they are turning at road junctions, this Oxford Diecast van and the bus in Fig. 297 have the front wheels re-set to a turned steering position.

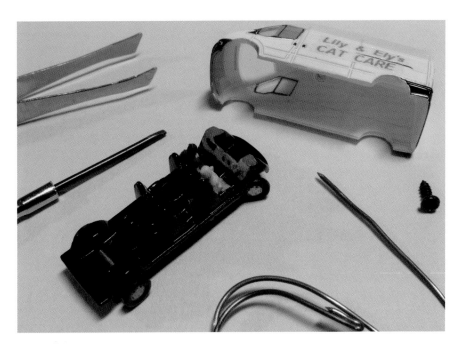

Fig. 276 The single screw is removed to free the van body from its chassis for the driver and passenger to be glued into their seats. Dashboard details are painted on, and copper wire is used to replace the steel axle for the front wheels to be re-set in the turned steering position.

are then bent in the turn position on the copper-wire axle and are sealed with superglue. Although it is feasible to instal drivers and other occupants in N-gauge cars, it is doubtful if they could easily be seen through the relatively tiny plastic glazed windows to make the extra work involved worth-while. Larger N-gauge vehicles, on the other hand, such as vans and buses, have larger windows through which occupants can be seen, especially if the vehicles are positioned towards the front of the layout. Commercially produced seated figures that are normally intended for platform seating may be too large to fit into van and bus seats. However, the legs of standing figures can be cut off with just the upper bodies glued into vehicle seats.

BOATS

Paddle-boarders are also included in this category, as they are essentially a basic boat. The paddle-boarders featured on the river basin are made from styrene sheet and are cut to the shape of surf boards with front ends curved upwards. Paddle-blades are also cut from thin styrene and are glued to shafts cut from plastic rod. Standing model-railway figures are adapted by cutting their arms and

re-setting them to hold the paddle-blades, and the figures are glued to the paddle-boards, which are painted in bright colours, with the figures painted mainly black to represent wet suits. The paddle-boarders are glued to the surface of the water with clear-water effects gel, which is also used to create the ripple effects on the water a small paintbrush. Other craft in the river basin consist of white metal mouldings of inflatable dinghies and an old-style rowing boat, converted to a sailing boat by adding a mast made from plastic rod and rigging using nylon fishing-line. The white metal mouldings are painted by first removing any moulding flash with a file and applying a paint primer undercoat, followed by a coat or two of Humbrol enamel.

Scratch-built canal-type pleasure craft are also featured. Being fundamentally box-shaped, these craft are straightforward to build from balsawood and styrene sheets. All three canal craft in the river basin share the same method of construction; the only difference is that the larger craft has an additional window and a porthole on each side of the cabin. The construction sequence for these craft is shown in numerical order in Fig. 280 and described in Steps 1–9.

Fig. 277   Paddle-boarding by moonlight. Ripple effects are created with Woodlands Scenics water-effects gel. Details on how to construct the canal boats are shown in Fig. 280.

Fig. 278   This canal cruiser has handrails on the roof and a door opening cut out in the bulkhead, with cabin doors and hatch glued in the open position, constructed from styrene sheet. The bicycle and figures are produced by Preiser.

Fig. 279 *The outboard motorboat is carved from balsawood.*

Boats

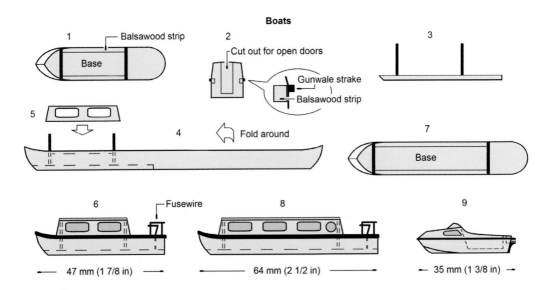

— 47 mm (1 7/8 in) — — 64 mm (2 1/2 in) — — 35 mm (1 3/8 in) —

Fig. 280 *Canal boat bases and bulkheads are cut out from 1.5mm ($^1/_{16}$in) styrene sheet, hull sides are cut from paper-thin styrene. Cut out the cabin doorway in the aft bulkhead for the open-door option before gluing the bulkhead to the base of the canal boat. Fibre-optic cabin lighting is glued from beneath the layout, through the bottom of the hull, into a balsawood table before the roof is glued to the cabin sides.*

Steps 1 and 2

Trace and cut out the three canal-craft bases and bulkheads. The bulkheads are the same size for all three canal boats.

Step 3

Glue the bulkheads to the bases.

Step 4

Trace and cut out the hull sides and wrap and glue them around the base and bulkhead sides. Glue a balsawood strip along the top inside edge of the hull sides between the bulkheads to strengthen the hulls.

Step 5

Trace and cut out the cabin sides and windows and glue the sides to the top of the hulls and bulkhead sides.

Step 6

Glue clear acetate-sheet window glazing to the inside of the cabin sides prior to gluing on the roofs. (For illuminating the insides of the cabins, refer to Fig. 297.) Construct the aft handrail and tiller arm from household fusewire.

Steps 7 and 8

The construction details of the larger canal craft are shown in Fig. 280.

Step 9

The outboard motorboat is carved from balsawood with the cockpit and engine well hollowed out. Balsa cement is smeared over the hull and cabin to seal the grain and smoothed with glasspaper prior to painting. The outboard motor is constructed from styrene sheet, including the windscreen fairing, forward hatch and hull gunwale strakes.

Fig. 281   The tourist attraction is an Airfix MkI Spitfire plastic mini-kit showing the open cockpit conversion.

AN AEROPLANE

Perhaps not the usual model railway accessory to include on a layout. I initially considered stringing an aeroplane on a nylon line across the back of the layout, reminiscent of my boyhood days when poorly painted, dust-laden plastic kits of aircraft were suspended from my bedroom ceiling. However, I do not think a suspended inert propeller-driven-type aircraft really cuts it in the realism stakes.

A stationary aircraft on the ground, on the other hand, would, I thought, make an unusual tourist attraction for a model train layout, and would also be an excuse to partly satisfy my interest in all things aeronautical. Coincidentally, Airfix produce mini-plastic kits of aircraft, which are near N-gauge size, including the iconic WWII Spitfire, which caught my attention when deciding to make an aircraft kit into a static tourist attraction. The standard plastic kit of the Spitfire is supplied with the cockpit canopy moulded in the closed position and I thought it would be a neat idea to show the cockpit with the canopy in the open position to show a pilot seat and control column. The canopy is cut in half with a razor saw and the top of the fuselage is cut away between the windscreen position and the rear half of the canopy to provide the opening for the cockpit. The pilot seat is constructed from scrap styrene

and glued to a false floor, which is in turn glued to the inside of the fuselage on a supporting block of rigid foam. The drop-down pilot access panel in the port side of the fuselage is made by cutting out a panel using a razor saw and knife, and gluing the cut-out panel to the fuselage in the open position. A control column, which is glued into the false floor in the cockpit, is made from household fusewire by bending the top of the column around a pin to form the circular hand-grip. Seat harness straps are cut from a strip of tan-coloured painted paper, glued to the seat back. Finally, the windscreen and the rear half of the canopy are glued in the open position to the fuselage. The model is painted as stated in the instructions supplied with the kit, and the model glued by its undercarriage to the layout with yellow-painted wheel chocks, cut from styrene strip, glued on each side of the undercarriage wheels.

DETAILING THE BUILDINGS AND STRUCTURES

BUILDINGS

Some of the building details have already been described in Chapter 6, and to summarize include: attaching satellite dishes and drain pipes, and high-

Fig. 282 Pva glue is applied into the gap at the bottom of the garage base.

Fig. 283   Fine sawdust or landscaping foliage is sprinkled on top of the glue to hide the gap.

lighting individual stones, mortar courses and roof slates using different shades of paint. In addition, one of the more noticeable improvements that can be made is where buildings are mounted on the layout leaving an unwanted visible gap between the base of the building and the ground. This is particularly noticeable with internally illuminated buildings, whereby light can be seen through the gap, which was the case with the car-repair garage when it was first installed. There are two methods I have found to hide any unsightly gaps. The first method is either to fill the gap with acrylic filler or to use glue-soaked sawdust, which is then painted over to represent dirt to help the base of the building to blend in with the ground. The other method is to sprinkle landscaping foliage over glue, which is applied to the gap to represent grass or weeds. Where buildings and station platforms are screwed to the layout and require removing for access to

bulbs and wiring, for example, the above gap-filling methods can still apply. When the glued gap has set, slide a razor blade between the building and the layout to produce a hairline joint.

STRUCTURES

Structures on the layout include bridges, station platforms and fences. The arched stone-effect road bridge is detailed with dabs of green foliage-coloured paint, applied with a small brush to represent grass between the stonework. Patches of general dirt and grime are applied by lightly marking surfaces with an HB-grade pencil and smudging the pencil marks with your finger until the required result is achieved. This method is also applied to the stone-effect viaduct and the road bridge with some of the individual embossed stones highlighted with lighter and darker shades of stone-coloured paint. The two plate-girder bridges and footbridges are

Fig. 284 Shade on smoke, dirt and grime effects on bridges with a soft pencil; use dabs of green paint for moss on the bridges.

Fig. 285 Repair patches on the platform are replicated with matt-grey paint and black pitch lines marked on using a marker pen. A white colour wash is brushed over the top of the patches. Rusty areas on railings are lightly brushed on matt-brown paint. Yellow platform lining is a self-adhesive vinyl strip, available in rolls from the Hobby's catalogue, and is protected by painting a clear, matt varnish over the top.

also weathered with wear-and-tear effects marked on with a pencil, including painting rust patches using matt-brown paint.

Station platform surfaces are detailed with patches of repair work, represented by painting a different shade of grey paint to that of the colour of the platform surface. The pitch-effect bordering around the patches is drawn on using a black marker pen with a thin, white colour wash applied over the top.

Metal-effect trackside spear fencing is supplied in strip form in shiny black plastic, which looks fine if it is intended to depict a new or freshly painted fence. However, it is probably more common to see this type of fencing in the real world with rusting railings

and flaking paint, which is replicated by lightly brushing matt-grey and rust-coloured paint onto selected areas of the fence.

White wood-style plastic trackside fencing is similarly supplied in strip form and can remain unpainted, or parts of the fencing can be weathered by lightly brushing on matt-grey paint and/or creating general dirt and grime effects using a pencil. For that neglected look, clumps of landscaping foliage are glued on to parts of the fence to represent grass and undergrowth. This is particularly useful to hide joints between lengths of fencing.

The track can arguably be termed as a structure, albeit a long, horizontal one. I have found painting the sides of the track rails an authentic rust colour

Fig. 286   Weathering wood-fencing with lightly applied brush strokes of matt-grey paint. Foam landscaping foliage is glued to fencing for that neglected look. Black metal and white wood-effect plastic fencing are produced by Ratio and Wills.

far easier to do before the track is laid, rather than having to bend over the layout attempting to hold the paintbrush steady with the track in situ on the layout. Nevertheless, the laid track will still benefit from additional detailing by painting some of the sleepers a grease and grime colour, particu-

larly in sidings and also on track alongside station platforms. Weeds and grass between the tracks are represented with clumps of glued-on foam land-scaping foliage, checking that it does not obstruct the passage of trains, especially on bends where long carriages overhang the track.

Fig. 287   Brushing on one of the specialized railway colours that are available from model railway shops, in this case an oil/grease colour on railway sleepers.

CHAPTER NINE

PHOTOGRAPHING SCENES AND DIORAMAS

LIGHTS – CAMERA – ACTION

While spending many a pleasurable hour building the layout, I thought it would be worthwhile not only to photograph my completed creation, but also to photograph some of the stages during its construction to show friends how I have spent my time. Photographs would also provide me with a permanent record to look back on when the layout is eventually rehomed, or ends up as firewood, perish the thought. A few photographs might also be useful for insurance purposes and to perhaps interest one or two model railway magazines or book editors who might be interested in publishing a feature on the layout. This book came about as a direct result of that process.

The photographs of the night and day scenes on the layout, as indeed all the photographs in the book, were taken using a compact digital camera featuring manual settings, as well as the usual

Fig. 288   The completed Teignside Quay standing on its bolt-on legs, ready to be photographed. A floor-standing and a desk-top tripod are must-have accessories for taking shake-free shots.

automatic photo-taking mode. One of the advantages of using a compact camera is that it can be placed in positions directly on the layout where this would otherwise be difficult to do with a larger type of camera, such as a digital SLR camera, especially on an N-gauge layout. Apart from a suitable camera, a floor-standing tripod and a small desk-top tripod are useful. A couple of adjustable tabletop lamps fitted with daylight bulbs are also useful for photographing objects on a table. One lamp is placed on each side of the object to cancel out unwanted shadows. Natural daylight is the best source of light by which to take photographs, preferably from a north-facing window to avoid shadows. However, I have found that a camera that can compensate for artificial lighting will also give satisfactory results. Setting the flash mode on the camera should be avoided, if possible, as close-up shots will probably result in a 'washed-out' appearance. Depending on the camera's capability, and if there is adequate lighting, it is possible to take acceptable 'hand-held' shots with good depth-of-field focus using the camera's auto-mode setting when taking photographs from a little distance away from the object. For shots near ground level, the majority of the photographs, however, were taken using either a tripod or by placing the camera directly on the layout. In some cases photographs were taken with the camera balanced precariously on buildings, supported with scraps of foam and balsawood with the

Fig. 289   View from the bridge. Cars are attached to the roads with Blu-Tack permitting them to be relocated, if required. The metal-bodied bus is comparatively heavy and is mounted on a wood block, glued to the layout. A BR-lined green tank locomotive, produced by Dapol, pulling a Graham Farish BR Stanier coach, waits at Teignside Quay Station.

self-timer function engaged to avoid camera shake. The main camera setting that I usually use, apart from the manual focus function, is the 'aperture priority' mode to obtain the depth of field (range of sharpness) I require to ensure that the maximum amount of the subject is in focus. My camera, a Panasonic LX5 (other makes of camera are available), has an aperture range of between f/2 and f/8, with f/8 giving the greatest depth of field, and the f/2 setting used only to focus on an important part of a subject, while blurring the foreground or background, for example. Shutter speed and exposure time are automatically selected, depending on the light conditions. Typically, exposure times for the night shots were between 2 and 4sec with the self-timer function engaged to trigger the shutter. The 'macro' setting on the camera is used to photograph subjects a few millimetres away from the lens.

SCENIC VIEWS

Figures 289–298, with accompanying captions, show general views of the completed layout.

Fig. 290 All the trees, including the commercially produced deciduous trees, are given two coats of ordinary hairspray to bind and strengthen the foam foliage to the plastic armatures before the trees are mounted on the layout.

Fig. 291   Conifer-type trees, which are made using plastic tree armatures and foam foliage produced by Woodland Scenics, are ideal where space is at a premium, such as between tracks and on the station backscene. A Graham Farish A1 Class 'Tornado' is about to pull out from Teignside Station, while the diminutive diesel shunter takes a run up the incline on the preserved line.

Fig. 292   Art-quality card is used to construct the bridge deck and approach roads, which are glued to foam supports. A soft pencil is used to produce the dirt and grime effect at the base of the bridge abutment.

ABOVE: **Fig. 293** Road signs, including the 30mph signs on the approach road leading to the level-crossing, are from the Gaugemaster Tiny Signs range. Station names are typed using a computer in different sizes to obtain the correct size. These are then glued on to backing boards, cut from styrene sheet and glue-mounted on to plastic rod posts. The six-axle drive on the Graham Farish Class 57 diesel locomotive makes short work on the preserved line gradients.

BELOW: **Fig. 294** The N-gauge tram and associated catenary poles are produced by Kato. A photograph taken of the back of these terraced cottages is used for the side scene at the back of Teignside Station.

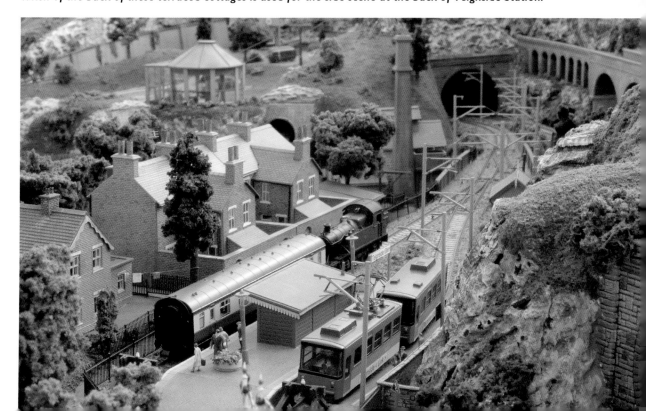

Fig. 295   Lighting adds another dimension to the layout, with street lighting, internally illuminated buildings, floodlit viaduct and manor house.

Fig. 296   The tram body is unclipped from the chassis of this Kato tram and an LED attached out of sight inside of the roof cab. It is wired into the motor circuit, with the driver figure glued to the chassis.

Fig. 297 The painted headlights on this Oxford Diecast model bus are drilled out and replaced with fibre-optic cable lighting. Bus wheels are reset to a steered turn position. The bus queue is from the PECO Modelscene budget range of unpainted figures. The cabin on the canal boat is also illuminated with fibre-optic cable, glued up through a cabin table, which is made from scrap card, before the cabin roof is glued into position. The bench table seating has a bulb wired to the underside of the parasol.

Fig. 298 Bulb lighting is fitted inside the cable-car buildings and the public house (spot the silhouette figure in the window). Floodlighting the cable cars is courtesy of an LED wired to the front of the main building.

DIORAMAS

It is said that 'less is more' and, therefore, rather than populate every corner and available space on the layout with a carpet of figures, I tried to concentrate mainly on creating small, individual scenes (dioramas). An example of this is depicted with the garage-repair scene in Fig. 221. Browsing online and thumbing through catalogues are a source of generating ideas for creating dioramas. Figures engaged in all manner of activities are available, such as track maintenance, weddings, fishing and cycling. Boats and vehicles are also offered, which can be used to form a centrepiece for a diorama setting.

Figures 299–305, with accompanying captions, show some of diorama scenes on the layout.

Fig. 299 The round tabletops are made from styrene clippings using a hole punch. Chairs are adapted from commercially produced platform seating, with the centre section cut out and the leg ends glued together. The potted plant is landscaping foliage glued into a cut section of aluminium tube, which forms the plant tub.

Fig. 300 One of the party revellers sits on the edge of a water feature, made from stone-effect styrene sheet, the inside of which is painted blue and filled with Woodland Scenics water-effects resin. The centre of the water feature is a fountain made from fibre-optic cable, connected to an LED mounted under the baseboard.

ABOVE: **Fig. 301** Commercially produced packs of figures produced by Preiser and Noch depict various activities, such as these building maintenance figures mending the roof. An Oxford Diecast model of the VW truck is weathered with grey paint and is loaded with building materials, cut from scrap plastic.

BELOW: **Fig. 302** The small maintenance yard is created using a plastic kit of a lineside hut. The pile of track ballast chippings and sandy ground are held in place with diluted pva glue dribbled over the top.

Fig. 303   The stonework on this derelict lineside building is created from individual OO-scale track ballast chippings glued on to card. The collapsed roof rafters are strips of painted balsawood, covered with weeds using landscaping foliage.

Fig. 304   An Oxford Diecast Land Rover launches the Langley Models white metal inflatable dinghy, converted into a sports powerboat with the addition of a seated helm console and lighting gantry, using scrap styrene and household fusewire.

Fig. 305   The A1 Class 'Tornado' passing over one of the Peco plate-girder bridges, weathered with rust patches represented with brown paint. The lone figure is from the Noch range of figures.

CHAPTER TEN

LIGHTING EFFECTS

LED FLOODLIGHTING

The viaduct and manor house are externally illuminated with uplighting using 3mm LEDs mounted at the base of these structures. The sides of the LEDs are shielded from view by inserting them in aluminium tubing, which is painted grey. Two green-coloured LEDs are used for lighting the manor house, with three blue-coloured LEDs to illuminate the viaduct. To achieve the desired lighting effect, the LED uplighters are connected and switched on while positioning them on the baseboard and substructure, and lightly glued in place so that they can easily be repositioned or replaced, if required.

Fig, 306 *Green LED uplighters illuminating the front of the manor house are concealed behind the terrace wall. The central pond feature and palm tree sculpture are created from glued-together and bent lengths of 0.75mm-diameter fibre-optic cable, while 0.5mm fibre-optic cable is used for lights on top of the wall pillars. The station footbridge is illuminated with a couple of bulbs attached inside the roof.*

Fig. 307   Blue LED uplighters are positioned at the base of each viaduct column and near the base of the rock face.

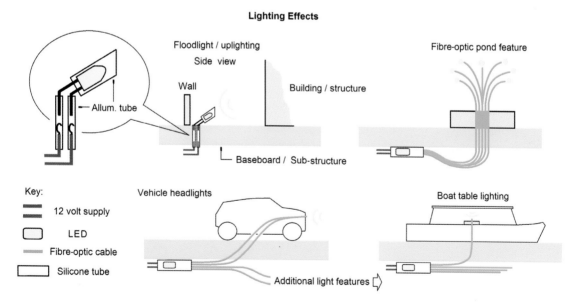

Lighting Effects

Floodlight / uplighting
Side view

Wall

Allum. tube

Building / structure

Baseboard / Sub-structure

Fibre-optic pond feature

Key:

▬▬ 12 volt supply

▭ LED

▬ Fibre-optic cable

▭ Silicone tube

Vehicle headlights

Additional light features

Boat table lighting

Fig. 308   For the lighting effects, 3mm LEDs are used for the uplighters and to provide light to the fibre-optic cables. The uplighter LEDs are connected through the baseboard to the 12V lighting wiring circuit with aluminium tubing. A 100K ohm resistor is soldered onto the positive feed wire to prevent the LED from burning out. Silicone tube is pushed over the LED to hold the ends of fibre-optic cables where these are used for vehicle and boat lighting.

FIBRE-OPTIC LIGHTING

Typically, the thickness of fibre-optic cables that is suitable for use in models ranges from 0.25mm to 2mm in diameter. The use of fibre-optic cables for lighting in cars, boats and the bus have already been described elsewhere in this book. However, there are other uses for this versatile lighting method, such as creating the illuminated pond feature and palm tree sculpture in the grounds of the manor house. Both these features are illuminated from an LED mounted under the baseboard with 0.75mm diameter fibre-optic cables being threaded up through the baseboard and sub-structure. Additional points of light are provided on top of the pillars at the front of the manor house and on bollards adjacent to the river basin, using smaller-diameter fibre-optic cables with an additional LED.

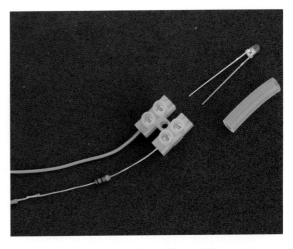

Fig. 309 Items required for LED and fibre-optic lighting: LED, screw-type connecting block (or aluminium tubing can be used); 100K ohm resistor and silicone tube.

LEFT: **Fig. 310 Illuminated pond feature.** The tips of the 0.75mm fibre-optic cables, available from the Hobby's catalogue, are bent outwards and the ends pushed into the other end of the silicone tube, which has adhesive tape wrapped around it to prevent light loss.

RIGHT: **Fig. 311 About two-dozen lengths of 0.25mm-diameter fibre-optic cables** can be packed into the end of the silicone tube to provide individual points of light from a single 3mm LED.

Fig. 312 Fibre-optic headlights on the worked-on car complement the illuminated garage, which is fitted with a workbench and tools made from wire and scrap styrene.

CHAPTER ELEVEN

BACK IN THE BOX

Fig. 313 The clearance of landscaping features is occasionally checked with the layout closed as construction progresses.

This is where things can get interesting, especially if the layout has not been checked during the landscaping stage to see that it can be folded and closed without mishap to the layout within – although the tops of the odd fir tree or two are easily pruned to prevent them from impaling themselves in some part of the other half of the layout. Obviously, anything that is not glued down, screwed or fixed to the layout must be removed before folding the layout. This includes unplugging and removing the train controller, disconnecting the layout joint electrical connections, unclipping and removing the suspended cable cars and checking that no forgotten locomotives or rolling stock are left hidden in the tunnels. It is surprising with just a modest-sized layout, such as Teignside Quay, how the total weight can be considerable even though featherweight light foam is used for the baseboard and sub-structure. It is, therefore, suggested that the two halves of the layout are unbolted first and carried separately if any distance is involved in transporting the layout. Where the layout is to be stored in a cupboard at home, for example, the layout can be tilted and gently walked from side to side on its plastic feet across the floor, or carried by two persons to its intended location. Alternatively, a 12mm (½in) plywood base can be cut out, with a heavy duty furniture castor screwed to each corner, upon which the folded layout can stand and be wheeled about.

I am sometimes asked how long the layout took to build and I guess, dear reader, this question is also on your mind. To be matter of fact about it, my answer is that it has taken me approximately 3,000 hours to build, spread over a leisurely six years. Most of this time was spent on constructing the landscaping and scratch-building the working features. However, I think the amount of time building the layout is of little consequence compared with the pleasure it has given me, and will also perhaps be the same for you, if you decide to design and build your own folding layout, or indeed build Teignside Quay.

Figs 314 and 315   When not in use, the closed layout could double up as a coffee table with a polished wood panel placed on top, or stored away in a cupboard under the stairs.

REFERENCES AND FURTHER READING

In addition to what appears to be a galaxy of websites to choose from for information on model railways, magazines also offer an excellent source of reference, and include featured layouts, 'how to' articles and up-to-date product reviews. Magazines that are generally available from newsagents and by subscription include: *Continental Modeller, Hornby Magazine, Model Rail, Model Railroader, British Railway Modelling (BRM)* and *Railway Modeller*.

The following books and publications are available online or from book and model shops:

Appleton, Paul (ed.) *Model Railway Design Manual* (Hornby, 2014)
Bardsley, I. *Making a Start in N Gauge Railway Modelling* (Crowood, October 2013)
Bardsley, I. *Planning and Making Railway Layouts in Small Spaces* (Crowood, January 2013)
Burkin, N. *Model Railway Layout, Construction and Design Techniques* (Crowood, June 2010)
Flint, Steve (ed.) *Your Guide to Railway Modelling* (Peco, 2013)
Marriott, P, *Railway Modelling Skills* (Crowood, 2015)
Peco *Railway Models and Publications* (Peco, March 2012)
Rice, I. *Railway Modelling the Realistic Way* (Haynes, December 2007)

USEFUL WEBSITES

Websites of companies where model railway items and materials were obtained for constructing the layout featured in this book:

Graham Farish
Locomotives, rolling stock, buildings and figures
www.grahamfarish.co.uk

Peco
Publications, track, rolling stock and buildings kits
www.peco-uk.com

Gaugemaster
Model railway-related items
www.gaugemaster.com

Hindleys
Styrofoam
www.hindleys.com

E.M.A. Model Supplies
Scenic materials, Styrofoam, sheet plastics, motors, gears and pulleys
www.ema-models.com

Woodland Scenics
Landscaping materials and water effects resin
www.woodlandscenics.com

Maplin Electronics
Plugs and sockets, switches, wiring and LEDs
www.maplin.co.uk

Ratio and Wills
Buildings and lineside items plastic kits, stone-effect styrene sheets
Available via the Peco website: www.peco-uk.com

Metcalfe
Printed card buildings kits and printed stone- and brick-effect card and paper sheets
www.metcalfemodels.com

Jordan
Cork bark
www.modelscenerysupplies.co.uk

W. Hobby Ltd
Geared electric motors, gear cogs, fibre-optic cable and materials
www.hobby.uk.com

Technobots
Electric motors and gears
www.technobotsonline.com

Faller
Buildings plastic kits
Available via the Gaugemaster website:
www.gaugemaster.com

Hornby
Model railway-related items
www.hornby.com

Kato
Locomotives
Trams, track, buildings and lineside items
www.wellingtonmodels.com and via the Gaugemaster website: www.gaugemaster.com

Preiser, Wiking, Busch, Noch and Modelscene
Figures and vehicles
Available via Gaugemaster website:
www.gaugemaster.com

Oxford Diecast
Vehicles
www.oxforddiecast.co.uk

Langley Models
White metal and ready-painted boats, vehicles, figures, buildings and accessories
www.langleymodels.co.uk

Quasar Electronics
Sound and message recorder modules, electronic kits
www.quasarelectronics.co.uk

Airfix
Aircraft plastic kits
www.airfix.com

Dapol
Locomotives
www.dapol.co.uk

Rapid Electronics Ltd
Electronic components, connectors and mechanical fastenings
www.rapidonline.com

MISCELLANEOUS WEBSITES

Expressway Models
South Devon Heritage Railway, Buckfastleigh Station
Model railway-related items and advice
www.southdevonrailway.co.uk

N Gauge Society
Promotes N-gauge model railways and provides a forum for enthusiasts
www.ngaugesociety.com

New Railway Modellers
Dedicated to beginners, offers advice on all aspects of model railways
www.newrailwaymodellers.co.uk

Model Rail Forum
News, reviews and resources
www.modelrailforum.com

INDEX

RELATED TITLES FROM CROWOOD

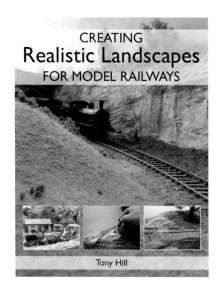

**Creating Realistic Landscapes
for Railway Modellers**
TONY HILL
ISBN 978 1 84797 219 4
160pp, 400 illustrations

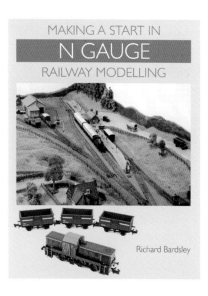

**Making a Start in N Gauge
Railway Modelling**
RICHARD BARDSLEY
ISBN 978 1 84797 556 0
192pp, 300 illustrations

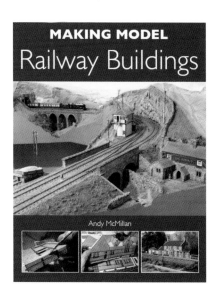

Making Model Railway Buildings
ANDY McMILLAN
ISBN 978 1 84797 340 5
288pp, 620 illustrations

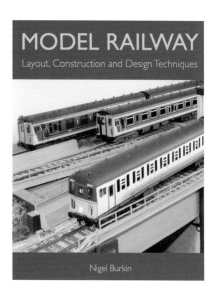

**Model Railway Layout, Construction
and Design Techniques**
NIGEL BURKIN
ISBN 978 1 84797 181 4
192pp, 340 illustrations

RELATED TITLES FROM CROWOOD

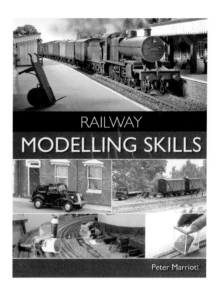

**Planning, Designing and Making Railway
Layouts in Small Spaces**
RICHARD BARDSLEY
ISBN 978 1 84797 424 2
144pp, 130 illustrations

Railway Modelling Skills
PETER MARRIOTT
ISBN 978 1 84797 955 1
224pp, 400 illustrations

In case of difficulty ordering, please contact the Sales Office:

The Crowood Press
Ramsbury
Wiltshire
SN8 2HR
UK

Tel: 44 (0) 1672 520320

enquiries@crowood.com

www.crowood.com